THE
PROBLEM
OF
THE
SELF

THE
PROBLEM
OF
THE
SELF

Henry W. Johnstone, Jr.

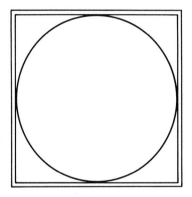

THE PENNSYLVANIA
STATE UNIVERSITY
PRESS

University Park & London

Copyright © 1970 by The Pennsylvania State University
All rights reserved

Library of Congress Catalog Card Number 71-84666
Standard Book Number 271-00102-X

The Pennsylvania State University Press
    University Park, Pennsylvania 16802
The Pennsylvania State University Press, Ltd.
    London, W.1, England

Printed in the United States of America
Designed by Marilyn Shobaken

For Margery,
my alter ego

*Der ausgeführte Zweck oder das
daseyende Wirklich ist Bewegung und
entfaltetes Werden; eben diese Unruhe
aber ist das Selbst.*—Hegel

CONTENTS

PREFACE

A long time ago I participated in an evening of philosophical discussion in the home of a colleague. When the evening was over, I came home in the company of two other colleagues who had also been involved in the discussion. One of them turned to the other and, referring to our erstwhile host, said, "He doesn't see that the self is a problem." This remark puzzled me. I was sure that my colleague did not mean merely that the self *posed* a problem. He meant that the self *was* a problem—that its nature was *to be* a problem. This book is an attempt to understand what it could mean to call the self a problem in this sense. In the course of writing it, I have come to agree with this characterization of the self, although, if pressed, I might prefer to identify the self as the *acceptance* of a problem. But in the more trenchant if more cryptic language of my former colleague, I would now wish to say that if there is a problem of the self, its solution is that the self is a problem. In the pages that follow I will give some reasons for supposing that this is the case.

Many friends and colleagues will see that I have either appropriately or inappropriately responded to their advice concerning the book as a whole or specific parts of it. I am indebted to all these people. Particular thanks are due Aaron Druckman, Richard Hocking, Robert Price, John E. Smith, and Carl Vaught, whose suggestions showed that they all understood much more clearly than I did myself what I was trying to do. Professor Gottfried Martin of the University of Bonn, and his *Doktoranden Kreis,* with whom I discussed parts of six chapters of the book, have given me substantial help with the final revision.

Some of the chapters of this book contain material that has already appeared in print. I wish to thank the editors of *Philosophy and Phenomenological Research, Logique et Analyse, The Proceedings of the 7th Inter-American Congress of Philosophy,* and *Kant-*

studien, respectively, for permission to use versions of "Persons and Selves," "On the Tall Napoleon," "On Wittgenstein on Death," and "Controversy and the Self."

The Central Fund for Research at The Pennsylvania State University supported much of the work that went into this book. James S. Morgan assisted me with research at the early stages. My appointment as Liberal Arts Scholar during the Spring Term of 1964 was a great help, and a Sabbatical during the first six months of 1968 was indispensable.

I am grateful to my daughter Anne for typing the manuscript. The index was prepared by Joan Kirshner.

H. W. J., Jr.

State College, Pennsylvania

1 · COMPUTERS AND PERSONS

Are you aware that the majority of the world . . . claim that many people know the things which are best, but do not do them when they might?—Plato

In this age of computers, it is both appropriate and convenient to begin a discussion of the concepts of person and self by asking whether a computer could ever be a person or have a self. The attempt to answer such questions helps to show, in a preliminary way, what sort of structure these concepts have. Even though my analysis of these concepts does not in the end depend upon any assumptions concerning computers, reflection on the properties and capacities of computers will help to orient the discussion.

It is important to emphasize that I am talking specifically about computers, not about machines in some indefinitely extended sense. For all I know, machines could be constructed sufficiently similar to persons to *be* persons. Such a robot might be made of synthetic flesh and blood, differing from a human being only in the way in which it was produced. To deny the possibility of machines of this kind is to take the position that man cannot be the maker of man. This is a theological thesis that is altogether independent of any argument I shall use in this book.

By a computer I mean any device that accepts data (such as numbers, for example) and, on the basis of certain instructions for processing these data, produces other data (numbers would again be an example). The data fed into the computer are called its *input,* the instructions for processing these data make up what is called its *program,* and the data the machine produces are called its *output.* Now it may be objected that in defining a computer in this fashion I have just surrendered any possibility of distinguishing a computer from a person. For a person can be regarded as a device that accepts data (not necessarily numbers, but sometimes sensory data), follows instructions for processing (i.e., interpreting) these data, and as a result produces output consisting of behavior (rather than necessarily numbers). I hope I can make it clear, however, not only in this opening chapter but throughout the book as a whole, that there are things persons can do that computers cannot do even if persons can also do what computers can do.

Notice that I have not defined a computer in such a way that a given input uniquely determines the output. Computers can be indeterministic as well as deterministic. They can be indeterministic in two different ways. It is possible, in the first place, deliberately to program a computer in such a way that one and the same input can result in various outputs. Since most programs, however, are not of this nature, most computers are not indeterministic in this way. In another way, however, they all are. As a physical device, any computer is fallible. Short circuits can develop, punching devices can stick, electronic parts can malfunction. Thus even though we may know what output, in theory, a computer ought to have if we provided it with a certain input and program, we can never be sure that it will in fact have this output.

Computers can to a considerable extent signal their own malfunctioning. In addition to the electronic devices involved in executing their programs, they usually contain auxilliary devices that report failures of various kinds. Thus, for example, a computer can compare its own program with the steps it has taken to execute it, and display a warning signal if there is any discrepancy. My argument will concern signals of this kind as well as the work that computers do in executing their programs.

I turn now to the question whether a computer could ever be a person or have a self. I will argue that if a computer ever signaled that it had through its own fault failed to do something it knew it had to do, the message would be false. But a person can truly signal that he has through his own fault failed to do something that he knows he had to do. It follows that a person cannot be correctly analyzed as a kind of computer. This conclusion is not intended as a contribution to the voluminous literature dealing with the question whether a computer can think.[1] I am not concerned with the question whether one or another of a person's intellectual skills can

1. For a bibliography up to mid-1962, see Feigenbaum and Feldman, *Computers and Thought*, New York, McGraw-Hill, 1963, pp. 477–523.

be duplicated by the machine. Of course, it is possible to construe a person's ability to take the blame as itself an intellectual skill; but if so, I do not believe that this skill has as yet been touched on in the literature.

People do sometimes take the blame for mistakes, and sometimes they are right to do so. A person can properly take the blame for a mistake under relatively trivial circumstances as well as in situations of moral importance. Thus, for example, the operator of a keypunch machine can take the blame for failing to supply a right-hand parenthesis that is needed to match a certain left-hand parenthesis. He may express his acceptance of the blame by saying "Confound it! I knew I should have put that parenthesis in!" This utterance is more than just an exclamation, since it can be false. It is false if the keypunch operator had not in fact known that the parenthesis was needed. The utterance again is at least inappropriate if the operator had known that the parenthesis was needed but the omission had occurred through no fault of his own. (It might, for example, have resulted from a malfunction in the keypunch machine itself.) It is inappropriate in this case to say "Confound it! I knew I should have put that parenthesis in!" because this utterance presupposes a false proposition—the proposition, namely, that the error was the operator's fault. Since whatever presupposes a false proposition is itself false, I conclude that the exclamation is not only inappropriate but false. It is on the other hand true if the operator knew that parentheses must be paired and that the omission could not in fact be ascribed to any agency but his own. We need not, of course, insist on the first of these conditions. The operator might know only that every character appearing on a sheet of paper had to be copied out on the machine, and see that the right-hand parenthesis was one of the characters. He could then properly take the blame if the malfunction were in fact his, not the machine's.

That a keypunch operator can know that he is to supply a right-hand parenthesis and yet fail to supply it when the time comes is an example of the age-old contradiction, first dealt with by Socrates, that apparently a person can know the right and do the wrong. In the present situation the contradiction is that the keypunch operator cannot imagine how he could have grasped more completely the need for the parenthesis, or how he could have been better prepared to supply it when the time came. If he did not know, how can anyone know anything? Yet his failure shows that he did not in fact know: he was not fully prepared. In one and the same sense of "know," and at one and the same time, the operator knew and did not know.

Of course there are distinctions that could sometimes save us from this contradiction. The situation might be analyzed in any of the following ways: (1) The operator was all set to put in the parenthesis, but his finger slipped. (2) He had once known about the parenthesis, but he forgot. (3) He knew that you must put in left-hand parentheses, but he did not know about the right-hand ones. In each of these cases it could plausibly be argued that the failure was not really the fault of the operator.

It may be a great comfort to the keypunch operator to be handed all these excuses. But it may not be. For he is the only person who can waive all excuses and simply take the blame. Once the error is pointed out to him—perhaps by means of a diagnostic message from a computer—his acceptance of the blame may well take the form of the exclamation I have attributed to him. He may simply say "Confound it! I knew I should have put that parenthesis in!"

The question to which I now turn is whether the contradiction of knowing the right and doing the wrong ever applies to a computer. A prior question, of course, is whether a computer can know anything at all. There are two important senses, I think, in which a computer can be said to know something. In the first of these senses its knowledge is identified in terms of its program; in the second it is evinced by its output.

I turn to the first sense. While ordinary language may not be the only source of evidence relevant to philosophical analysis, it does often point to distinctions and urgencies that need philosophical elaboration. The language that people who work with and around computers use as they go about their everyday tasks is a clue to the nature of computers, and one to which philosophers have rarely been attentive. Computer programmers and operators, for example, frequently speak of what a machine "knows." If a computer is programmed to treat the variables M and N as integers, it is said to know that M and N are integers, and if it is programmed to multiply M and N it is said to know that M and N are to be multiplied. Programmers often use locutions of this kind in analyzing the behavior of a machine as it executes a certain program. They may say, for instance, "Because the machine knows that M and N are integers, it treats M times N as an integer." One may, of course, object that the programmer who talks this way is using the word "know" carelessly or metaphorically. But who is to decide when it is being used judiciously and literally? Why should we not trust the programmer to use the word "know" correctly, at least in the sense in which he instinctively uses this word as he goes about his work?

Assuming then that being correctly programmed is at least one of the senses in which computers can know, I turn to the question whether they can properly take the blame for failing to do what they knew they were to do. Clearly, a computer can signal failure. No extension of current technology is required to equip a machine with a Multiplication Check Light. This light goes on whenever the machine has failed to carry out a multiplication it was to have carried out. The question, then, is whether the lighting up of the Multiplication Check Light can ever be tantamount to a true statement by the machine to the effect that it has through its own fault failed to do something it knew it was to have done. Certainly, by means of the light the machine is expressing its failure to do *something*. But is it saying that it *knew* it was supposed to do the thing it has failed to do? Is it saying, in effect, "Confound it! I knew I should have multiplied M and N!"? If what it means for the machine to know that it is to multiply M and N is that it is correctly programmed to multiply M and N, and the machine is not malfunctioning, the Multiplication Check Light will not light up at all unless it is itself malfunctioning. In this case, the lighting up of the light, if taken to express the proposition that the machine has failed to do something it knew it was to do, is a false alarm, just as would be the utterance of a person who said "Confound it! I knew I should have put that parenthesis in!" immediately after putting in the very parenthesis in question. If the machine is correctly programmed to multiply M and N and the Multiplication Check Light is not malfunctioning but still goes on, the computer must be malfunctioning in some part other than light. Can we in this case interpret the lighting of the light to mean "Confound it! I knew I should have multiplied M and N!"? Since the entire program is correct, it seems unreasonable to deny that the machine *knows* that it is to multiply M and N. The exclamation, however, is still inappropriate, just as is the exclamation of a keypunch operator who says "Confound it! I knew I should have put that parenthesis in!" even though the real trouble is that the keypunch machine itself is failing to respond to the parenthesis key. Such a person would be making a false statement, even though he might not know it to be false. He would be taking the blame for something that was not his fault. Similarly, if we interpret the lighting up of the Multiplication Check Light on a correctly programmed but malfunctioning computer to mean "Confound it! I knew I should have multiplied M and N!" we are supposing that the machine is taking the blame for something that is not its fault, so that its report is false.

The knowledge of a computer might be construed in terms of output as well as in terms of program. By this I mean that the machine might be programmed in such a way that it would behave knowingly under certain conditions. It might, for example, be programmed to duplicate what is essential to the behavior of the keypunch operator in saying "Confound it! I knew I should have put that parenthesis in!" To do this properly, it would have to convince us that it both knew it was supposed to perform a certain task and accepted the blame for failing to perform the task.

We can reduce to a minimum what is essential to the behavior of the operator by setting up an experiment of the sort Turing once proposed.[2] A person is in one room and a computer in another, and each can communicate with a second person (in a third room) only through a teleprinter. On the basis of his conversations via the two teleprinters, this second person is to decide which of his interlocutors is the person and which the computer. If messages like "Confound it! I knew I should have put that parenthesis in!" begin coming through the teleprinter, the decision may be very difficult, and the wrong one can easily be made. But the possibility of committing the error of identifying the computer as a person does not prove that it is a person. A person is not merely something that behaves like a person. A computer might dupe us into believing it was a person piteously pleading for his life. Once we saw that it was actually a computer, however, we would not hesitate to turn off the switch. Similarly, a computer might dupe us into believing that it was taking the blame for failing to do something it knew it was to do. But once we knew that it was a computer, we would see that its expressions of chagrin were no more than cleverly arranged output.

Of course, one can also be duped by a person expressing chagrin.

2. A. M. Turing, "Computing Machinery and Intelligence," *Mind*, Vol. 59, 1950, pp. 433–60.

But the way we are duped is not the way we are duped by the computer. When we see that a person has duped us we continue to see him as a person. When we see that a machine has duped us we no longer regard it as a person. It is not because we suddenly see the expression of chagrin as mere output from the person's brain that we become disenchanted, for this revelation would provide no basis for distinguishing real from sham chagrin. We are duped by a person's expression of chagrin when that expression is only a piece of play-acting. When it is more than only a piece of play-acting, the chagrin is real. If we could not make the distinction between sham and real chagrin, there would be no chagrin-like quality that we could mistakenly attribute to the computer.

It might be objected that the point at issue is not whether the computer can be chagrined but rather whether it can truly report that it has failed to do something it knew it had to do. Perhaps such a report can be appropriate output even when chagrin cannot. Yet chagrin, or something like it, is quite essential to the credibility of the report. If the statement "I knew I was to have done X, but I did not do it" has no emotional aura or overtone at all, it sounds like a blatant contradiction. How could anyone really *know* that he was to do X and yet not do it? We automatically invent distinctions that permit us to understand the statement as other than a contradiction: the person knew he was to do X, but forgot, or his finger slipped. A speaker's chagrin does not resolve the contradiction, but it does seem to make it more tolerable.

If chagrin cannot be appropriate output, how was it plausible at all to interpret the Multiplication Check Light as expressing "Confound it! I knew I should have multiplied M and N!"? The answer is that the light actually reported an internal state of the machine; it did not merely attempt to reproduce the behavior of someone reporting an internal state. It is easy to interpret the report of an internal state as chagrined even when the state itself is not that of chagrin, but it is impossible to interpret output as a chagrined report once we are convinced that there is no internal state at all of which it is a report.

If the Multiplication Check Light can plausibly be taken to express what is expressed by the exclamation "Confound it! I knew I should have multiplied M and N!," while output duplicating this very exclamation cannot be taken to express what this exclamation expresses—at least once it is identified as output—it may seem obvious that we ought to rebuild the machine in such a way that the Multiplication Check Light is replaced by a printer capable of producing the exclamation in question. For if the Multiplication Check Light directly reveals an internal state of the machine, it might be argued, so would the message printed by a printer connected to the machine in this way. Hence the message cannot be identified as mere output. Like the behavior of a person, it is behavior expressing an internal state.

This argument, however, makes a false assumption; namely that the *message* printed by an output printer could have the same function as the lighting of the Multiplication Check Light. In fact, it is not the message at all that would have this function if the machine were rebuilt in the manner indicated; it is just the *activity* of the printer. Whenever the printer began to clatter, the clattering itself would reveal precisely what is revealed by the Multiplication Check Light. Of course, we might want indications of various troubles over and above the failure to carry out a multiplication, in which case the appearance of different messages at the output printer would help us to distinguish the troubles. Such messages would correspond to a panel of lights, each indicating a different trouble. In place of each of these lights we might have used a separate output printer with its own recognizable clatter. The use of a single printer capable of producing various messages allows us to economize. The messages in effect constitute different clatters. Hence it is not what any message *states* that reveals to us an internal condition of the machine. Indeed, once we focus on what is *stated* by the message "Confound it! I know I should have multiplied M and N!," rather than just accepting this message as a distinctive clatter, the spell cast by the Multiplication Check Light or by the clatters as pure clatters will be broken. For what the message *states* is that some one individual both knew that he was to do something and failed to do it. One and the same speaker is claiming both to have been unable to fail and to have failed. Any computer operator or programmer would immediately see the message as the product of the activation of at least two distinct components of the machine: the component that was properly programmed to carry out the multiplication in question and the component that reported the failure to carry it out. He would see the two components as constituting, in effect, two distinct machines: a multiplying machine and a trouble-reporting machine. Hence his instantaneous response would be to see that the message is false when taken literally. It is false because there cannot be a *single component* that both knew it was to multiply M and N and reports its own failure to have done so. Once the programmer or operator perceives the falsity of the message, any spell it may have cast over him as a pure clatter will be broken; he will see that not even a Multiplication Check Light could in fact express what is expressed by "Confound it! I knew I should have multiplied M and N!" Perhaps, as an outcome of this nearly instantaneous sequence of reactions, the programmer or operator will comment that the message is "cute." This is his way of stigmatizing it once and for all as mere output.

A machine's behavior is "cute" when it imitates the behavior of a person. If no person could ever truly say "Confound it! I knew I should have multiplied M and N!" (or "put that parenthesis in") it is difficult to see what point there could be to imitating a person saying it. Be that as it may, when a person utters an exclamation like this, it is at least possible for there to be no difference between the "I" who knew and the "I" who reports the error. One and the same person can both know what he is to do and take the blame for not doing it. Persons are unified in a way in which machines are not. The unity of a machine is always provisional. We may be inclined to regard a computer with a single input card-reader as a unity. But if a Multiplication Check Light, or something like it, flashes on and is not itself malfunctioning, we immediately distinguish the machine's program, which is correct, from its circuitry, which is malfunctioning. If we receive the message "Confound it! I knew I should have multiplied M and N!" we immediately distinguish the part of the machine that knows it should have done the multiplication from the part that takes the blame. But in the case of the person we do not always make such distinctions; we do not always distinguish the part that is correct from the part that is malfunctioning, or the part that knew from the part that takes the blame for not doing what it was supposed to have done. The person himself who has committed the error can waive all proffered excuses. Others as well can sometimes see that he is to blame.

The unity of the machine, then, is provisional. Whenever it appears that the machine is engaged in contradictory behavior, of which one example would be knowing what to do but admitting failure to do it, its unity is immediately repudiated in favor of the presumption that the appearance has arisen from the conjoint behavior of at least two independently functioning components. This presumption is an instinctive execution of the injunction to make a distinction whenever we seem to see a contradiction. Implicitly supposing that there are no contradictions in nature, and unhesitatingly regarding the machine as a natural object, we naturally resolve any statement of the form "The machine is both P and non-P" by concluding that in one respect it is P and in another respect non-P.

Persons, however, sometimes exhibit a unity that is not merely provisional but is absolute. There are at least occasions on which a person correctly states that he knew what to do but failed to do it. To say that his statement is correct is to say that we cannot suppose that there are two distinct components, one of which knew and the other of which reports the failure. The use of the pronoun "I" often convinces us that one and the same agency both knew what to do and reports the failure. "I knew I should have put that parenthesis in!" is precisely a refusal on the speaker's part to accept any exculpatory distinction between a knower and a reporter of failure; and it is sometimes proper for a hearer to accept this refusal. The refusal is in effect the assertion that the "I" who knew is precisely the "I" who reports failure. It is also possible to blame *another* person for failing to do what he knew he should do even though the other has made no gesture toward taking the blame; and there are occasions on which such an act of blaming is correct. It is possible, in short, for the absolute unity of a person to prevent any distinction that would save us from contradiction.

The phenomenon of taking the blame for failing to do what one knew one was to do has traditionally been identified as guilt. Of course, one can feel guilt without *saying* anything (except possibly to oneself). One can also feel guilt over *doing* something that one knew was *not* to be done. Both of these extensions of the act of taking the blame *viva voce* for failing to do what one knew one was to do can readily be accommodated in the theory developed so far, which is to say that the machine is capable of manifesting neither. Machines cannot feel guilt, because their unity is only provisional. Only persons can feel guilt because only they can possess absolute unity.

It is important to state as clearly and candidly as possible that for me the concept of a person is a primitive concept. One does not observe a contradiction and accordingly infer the existence of a person. One must rather already be aware of the existence of a person in order to tell whether a contradiction of the relevant kind has been perpetrated. This point can be developed if we consider the obvious possibility of programming a machine to print out expressions syntactically defined as contradictions—there is no reason why "*p* and not-*p*" should not be the output of a computer. But while this output is syntactically a contradiction, no one would think that in producing it the machine was simultaneously asserting and denying one and the same proposition. A machine that merely *said* "I knew I was to put in that parenthesis and at the same time I did not know I was to put in that parenthesis" would not do at all as a counter-example to my contention that only persons can truly take the blame for not doing what they knew they should do.

It follows that the concept of contradiction of which I have been making use in this chapter is not merely a syntactical concept. It is rather a pragmatic concept, one that refers to the action of a person. It arises because a person not only can utter expressions which syntactically are contradictions but also can take deliberate steps toward justifying, from one and the same point of view, each side of such a contradiction. Such justification is not, of course, forthcoming from the machine that simply prints "*p* and not-*p*." Nor is it forthcoming from the machine that breaks down, on analysis, into two machines; for there is nothing in that situation to which we can ascribe a unified point of view.

One characteristic of a person is his capacity to issue contradictions of this pragmatic sort; and it is a characteristic that distinguishes the person from any machine. We must not imagine, however, that we could define the relevant sort of contradictions in the abstract without recourse to the concept of the person. Contradiction of the kind in question requires a unity that is to be found only in the person. The two concepts of person and contradiction are related in the indissolubly circular way that in philosophy is sometimes characterized as dialectical. Each presupposes the other.

Pragmatic contradictions are illustrated by what have in recent years been called "pragmatic paradoxes"—e.g., "I cannot speak any English." This statement becomes a contradiction only when I assert it. It remains innocuous so long as it is either unasserted or else asserted of me by someone else ("Johnstone speaks no English."). This latter situation is, of course, analogous to that of the machine, one part of which can innocuously say of another, "It has erred," but no one part of which can truly say "I have erred." Pragmatic paradoxes presuppose action on the part of a single agent; action in particular which denies or undercuts its own possibility. Paradoxes of this kind can always be avoided by positing a plurality of agents. Thus if "I cannot speak any English" is interpreted as the remark of a schizophrenic, meaning "That other person within me can speak no English," the paradox disappears.

The human condition has often been described as fraught with paradox. "Paradox," however, is somewhat too vague a word for my purposes. It has often been used to convey the idea of what is merely profoundly puzzling rather than actually self-contradictory. What I shall be interested in in this book, however, are genuine contradictions. Any such contradiction must be syntactically identifiable as such. In addition, it must arise pragmatically; that is, it must arise from the action of a single agent.

My argument so far has made use of the premise that a person can sometimes correctly say "Confound it! I knew I should have put that parenthesis in!" thereby taking the blame for failing to do something he knew he should have done. Since this premise is merely an appeal to ordinary language, it may not, however, be altogether convincing. In addition, it says nothing about the *necessity* of falling into contradiction. (A careful keypunch operator might never miss a parenthesis in his entire life.) This point is important because of the connection I will later try to establish between pragmatic contradictions and the self. The self *necessarily* arises only if pragmatic contradictions *necessarily* occur—only if they belong to the human condition. But a self arising only contingently could hardly be a proper topic for a philosophical study.

Both difficulties are resolved by the reflection that a statement in which I take the blame for failing to do something I knew I should have done is but one example of a broad class of statements, all of which are at root self-contradictory. The class includes all statements in which I ascribe any property to myself. Further examples are "I am tired," "I am hungry," "I am six feet tall." The distinctive feature common to all such statements is the claim that one and the same agent both has a certain property and reports it. If you say "I am tired," it is one identical person who *says* he is tired and *is* tired. This performance has no mechanical or logical model. If a machine ever said "I am tired," its provisional unity would break down into the duality of a reporting part and a tired part. But the unity of the person is powerful enough to fuse these parts into one, however inconsistent this fusion may be.

The phenomenon I have in mind is simply that of a person's self-reference. I shall return to it in Chapter 4.[3] It is clear, however, that a being incapable of referring to itself, or even a being which never in fact did refer to itself, could not be a person. Stripped of our powers of self-reference, we are stripped of our humanity. Of course, we need not use the first-personal pronoun; there exist other devices as well through which we can achieve self-reference—devices of which I will speak later. But a person must use *some* self-referential device; and it is in this sense that I regard self-reference, and hence contradiction, as necessary.

At the beginning of this chapter I raised the question whether a computer could be a person or have a self. So far I have discussed only the relation between computers and persons; I have said nothing directly about selves. In the next chapter I will turn to selves and will try to establish their relationship to persons. From that relationship it will be easy to devise an answer to the question about computers.

3. For an expansion of the remarks I have just made, see also my article "Persons and Selfreference," *Journal of the British Society for Phenomenology*, Vol. I, No. 1, 1970, pp. 46–54.

2 · PERSONS AND SELVES

Let them perish from Thy presence, O God, as perish vain talkers and seducers of the soul, those who, observing that in deliberating there were two wills, affirm that there are two minds in us of two kinds, one good, the other evil. . . . Myself when I was deliberating upon serving the Lord my God now, . . . it was I who willed, I who nilled, I, myself.—St. Augustine

Throughout the history of philosophy, there have been many views in which the self figures as a fundamental concept and many views in which the person figures as a fundamental concept, but there have been few views, if any, in which the self and the person have both been regarded as fundamental. For the views in which the self figures as a fundamental concept have usually treated the person as derivative (for example, as a mere composite of self and body), and the views in which the person figures as a fundamental concept have usually treated the self as derivative (for example, as a mere aspect of the behavior of the person) or else as altogether unnecessary. Yet there is no reason why self and person should not both be fundamental concepts. For they are entirely different in function. The concept of the person is, to use Heidegger's language, ontic; it does not arise from any theoretical concern.[1] Persons are directly encountered in everyday experience. On the other hand, the concept of the self is ontological; its genesis is theoretical. Except possibly for my own self, I never directly encounter selves; my awareness of them is indirect. The existence of the self is a sort of hypothesis used to explain the behavior of persons, but it is almost never as a hypothesis that we assert that a person exists.

1. It has been suggested that the concept of the person, *qua* concept, cannot be ontic. One who feels that this is a sound suggestion can substitute "nontheoretical" for "ontic" throughout what follows. My own feeling is that "ontic" is helpful, so I leave it.

Poe did frame the hypothesis that Maelzel's Chess Player was a person in order to explain its behavior.[2] This, however, is radically different from the hypothesis that a person has a self. If Poe was right, we could unlock the Chess Player, reach in, and pull out a human midget, thereby being directly confronted with a person. But no one who hypothesizes the self thinks that we could open a person, reach in, and pull out his self—the self is just not that sort of thing.

A view in which the person and the self are both fundamental is thus one which has a place for both ontic and ontological concepts. In this chapter I will outline such a view—one which is largely a development of the observation that the self is a hypothesis to explain the person.

I must emphasize, however, that there is almost never any need to invoke this hypothesis. For nearly everything that a person is and does can be adequately explained without appealing to the self. Why did Smith do that? Because he was frightened. Because Brown told him to. Because he wanted to earn some money. Because doing that made him happy. Because it reminded him of his childhood. Because he wanted to be the first to do it. None of these explanations contains any reference to Smith's self. In none of them would it make any sense to substitute "Smith's self" for "he" or "him." Even if Smith acted out of self-pity or self-esteem or to protect himself, there is no reference to Smith's self. When Smith acts out of self-pity, Smith simply acts out of pity for Smith. When he protects himself, he protects Smith.

What these explanations of Smith's conduct all have in common is that they belong to ordinary language. So, presumably, would the more technical explanations that might be given by the behavioral scientist or depth psychologist; for there is nothing extraordinary about technical language as such. Now ordinary language expresses ordinary experience and ordinary experience is ontic. (It may, of course, contain strata whose origins are theoretical; scientific constructs are often transformed in the course of time into immediate experience.) The fact that we can normally explain in terms of ordinary experience whatever there is about a person that seems to need explanation illustrates what I mean by calling the person an ontic concept. But although all ordinary

2. Edgar Allan Poe, "Maelzel's Chess Player," in the Raven Edition of *The Works of Edgar Allan Poe*, New York, P. F. Collier & Son, 1904, pp. 287–323.

experience is ontic, it does not follow that all ontic experience is ordinary. Even if the person is an ontic concept, a person can manifest extraordinary features that have no explanation in terms of ordinary experience or language. It is in such cases, and only in such cases, that we appeal to the self. The self, I shall argue, is the by-product of an unsuccessful attempt to apply the category of the ordinary to the person.

Views in which the person figures as a fundamental concept often neglect the point I have just made. Assuming that ontic experience is always ordinary, they conclude that nothing about the person is ever extraordinary, and hence that everything about the person can always be explained in terms of ordinary experience. Thus the self appears to be a gratuitous concept. In fact, we see the necessity of the self only when we admit that there can be something extraordinary about the person.

Something extraordinary about a person is something about him that cannot be explained in terms of ordinary experience. But what on earth is there that can*not* be explained in such terms? The answer is that since ordinary experience is governed by the Law of Noncontradiction, nothing genuinely self-contradictory about the person can be explained in terms of ordinary experience, although every consistent feature of the person can be so explained. Let me spell this answer out. To explain something in terms of ordinary experience is to give information about it that implies the feature we wish to explain; to explain Smith's behavior, for example, is to supply the information that he was frightened, that Brown told him to behave in that way, that he wanted to earn the money, or something else of the sort. A phenomenon that *in principle* cannot be explained in terms of information is thus one that in principle is not implied by any information that we could ever possess. But only an *inconsistent* phenomenon could be of this nature. Information cannot be inconsistent. What is consistent cannot imply what is inconsistent. Hence no information can imply an inconsistent phenomenon. And if a phenomenon is consistent, there is always information that implies it; to wit, the redundant information that it occurs. Thus for a phenomenon to be in principle inexplicable in terms of information, it is necessary and sufficient for it to be inconsistent.

In this chapter I will simply *assume* that persons can be genuinely inconsistent. Apart from considerations of the sort that

I adduced in Chapter 1, I would not know how to go about *proving* it. Any *literary* or *historical* example I could give could, of course, be questioned. If I said "Hamlet exemplifies inconsistent persons," someone would be sure to tell me that Hamlet was not really inconsistent. The reason why this outcome is certain has nothing to do with Shakespeare scholarship. It is rather that most people *presuppose* that no person is genuinely inconsistent. Hence when an alleged example of an inconsistent person is presented to them, they immediately invent a reason for supposing that the person in question was not inconsistent after all. I can avoid this reaction only by constructing my own example in which I *stipulate* an inconsistent person. Anyone who rejects my example on the ground that no person *can* be inconsistent thus begs the question. Of course *I* would beg the question if I thought my example constituted a *proof* that persons can be inconsistent.

To be sure, the keypunch operator of Chapter 1 might have served me as an example. In Chapter 1, however, I *argued* that this person was inconsistent. A reader who regarded that argument as unsound might well feel uncomfortable about accepting an invitation to *assume* that its conclusion is nevertheless true—that the operator is indeed inconsistent. It is better to begin now with a fresh example, and one to which argumentation is less relevant than it was to the characterization of the keypunch operator.

The example I will use is that of a person named Jones, who has both decided to go to a certain meeting and not decided to go. Jones is genuinely inconsistent. There is no saving distinction; we cannot say that in one respect he has decided to go but that in another respect he has not decided to go. For in all respects he has decided, and in all respects he has not decided to go. All the evidence points both ways.

This prefabricated example is not in fact very different from a literary example I might have used had I been willing to assume the risks; namely, that of Zerlina in Mozart's opera *Don Giovanni*. Her utterance "Vorrei e non vorrei"—"I would like to and I wouldn't"—spoken in answer to Don Giovanni's invitation to the summer house, expresses just the sort of inconsistency I have in mind. No saving distinction is indicated. The danger, of course, is that someone will immediately indicate one, telling me that Zerlina in one sense wanted to go but in another sense did not.

While I do not see how anyone who has listened to the opera could believe such nonsense, it would not only be beyond my qualifications but also totally irrelevant to get involved in a discussion of *Don Giovanni*. Hence I will stand by Jones, prosaic, hypothesized, and safe.

In discussing how the concept of the self is invoked by Jones's inconsistency, we have a choice between taking Jones's own point of view and taking that of an observer. There is some advantage in the latter approach, at least initially, since I do not wish to convey the impression that I regard Jones's self as something to which Jones has privileged access. Whatever Jones knows about his self, anyone else could in principle also know about it. Hence I reject the view, briefly mentioned earlier, that I can immediately encounter my own self in a way that I cannot encounter other selves.

I have already stated the role of Jones's self. It explains the inconsistency. Now usually when we meet an inconsistency, we explain it by explaining it away. We find a respect in which the thing in question has a certain property, and a contrasting respect in which it does not have it. But I have just said that Jones's inconsistency cannot be explained away in this fashion. Jones's self is not a respect of Jones. It is not a respect in which he has decided or not decided. How then, does it explain the inconsistency? Precisely by not explaining it away. Rather, the self is alleged to be the *locus* of the inconsistency, and hence explains it without repudiating it.

What it means to think of the self as the locus of an inconsistency can be put more concretely in terms of our example. If Jones has both decided and not decided, he is undergoing tension. We cannot give a correct account of Jones if we deny the existence of this tension. The tension presupposes simultaneous decision and failure to decide. If we said "In one respect Jones decided, but in another respect he failed to decide," we might be taken to mean that Jones has two selves—say, a true one and a false one—one of which decided while the other failed to decide. But this is a picture of schizophrenia, not of tension. One self has decided. There is no tension in it. Another self has not decided. There is no tension in it. Tension presupposes a *single* self, which has both decided and not decided. The schizophrenic alternation of true self and false self, as for example in Dr. Jekyll and Mr. Hyde, is in fact an evasion of tension. We see a person as undergoing tension only when we see him as having accepted both poles of a contradiction; that is, as having brought them within a single perspective.[3] This perspective is the person's self. It is the self that establishes the contradiction by bringing its poles together within a single perspective. Thus contradiction and self presuppose one another. In the absence of a self, there are no contradictions; there are at best evasive alternations of p and not-p. In the absence of a contradiction, there can be no self, for the self arises only on those occasions when the burden of a contradiction must be accepted. Contradiction, which calls the self into existence, presupposes that the self has already juxtaposed the contradictory poles. The self, in unifying the poles, establishes the very contradiction that evokes it. Where there is no self, no contradiction is acknowledged; the schizophrene is unaware of any difficulty in his position. Where there is no contradiction, no self arises; for there is then no need to appeal to any concept other than that of the person. The self is the *ratio cognoscendi* of the contradiction, and the contradiction is the *ratio essendi* of the self.[4]

I have distinguished between pragmatic and merely syntactical contradictions. Pragmatic contradictions are brought about through the action of a concrete person. It may be easier to visualize such action if we think of it as producing tension. Tension within the person is at least a pertinent example of a pragmatic contradiction.

We appeal to the self in order to account for the inconsistent person. In the case of someone other than ourself, we make this appeal as a kind of inference. Given the datum of the inconsistent person, we infer his self as the locus of the inconsistency. What we do, in effect, is to transfer an inconsistency from person to self. In the case of my own self, however, I hardly can be said to perform any such inference. I do not transfer an inconsistency from myself to my self; rather, in a single indivisible act I become aware of the inconsistency and of my self. My self *is* simply the acceptance

3. Of course, a person's simultaneous acceptance of two contradictory beliefs is not sufficient to establish that he is undergoing tension; he may merely be an expert at Orwellian "doublethink." Tension involves accepting a contradiction *and acknowledging that it is a contradiction.*
4. My colleague Robert Price points out that for the Ancients, who believed in the existence of the soul, contrariety is a mode of the association of ideas (together with similarity, contiguity, etc.; see Aristotle, *De Memoria et Reminiscentia);* whereas for modern philosophers who deny the existence of the soul (e.g., Hume), contrariety is not such a mode. Apparently, the soul is needed to bring the contrary ideas into juxtaposition.

of the inconsistency. But the contrast between the immediacy of my awareness of my own self and the mediacy of my awareness of another's self is not in any way a source of privilege; it is without epistemological importance. For I can be just as mistaken in supposing myself aware of my self as I can be in supposing myself aware of someone else's self. How such mistakes can arise I will indicate later.

The distinction between person and self is radical; they are not at all the same kinds of thing. The person is an individual. But it is not at all clear that the self is an individual. One is inclined to think of "self" as a bulk term like "money" or "water." We speak of some money and some water; why not also of some self? Some self emerges to take the burden of a contradiction. Of course we cannot prefix the name of any individual with "some" in this sense. There is an important difference, however, between "self" on the one hand and "money" and "water" on the other: there are cents and dollars of money and cups and gallons of water, but there are no units by which we measure the self. Another suggestion that may help us to see what kind of a concept we are dealing with is to think of the inconsistent Jones as being *selved*. To be selved is to have a property that cannot be subsumed under the category of the ordinary; it is to be afflicted with a problem. The difference between the adjectival force of the self and the non-adjectival force of the name of a person is one that Aristotle pointed out long ago: primary substance cannot be predicated of anything. In my view, the person is clearly an example of primary substance, but the self is not; indeed, it is doubtful that the self is a substance at all, in any of the Aristotelian senses.

Of course not every apparent contradiction involving a person calls up the idea of the person's self. If someone says that Smith is intelligent and someone else declares that Smith is unintelligent, this may mean simply that Smith is intelligent at mathematics but unintelligent in the conduct of business. If there seemed to be anything mysterious about Smith, surely this distinction dispels the mystery. A similar distinction might have sufficed to resolve "Jones decided to go but did not decide to go." Perhaps Jones decided to go, in the sense of physically betaking himself, but at the same time made it clear that his physical presence was not to be construed as an endorsement of a certain position. If this distinction can be made, there is no longer any contradiction to be transferred from the person Jones to Jones's self; the need for the idea of the self vanishes.

Let me try to spell out the conditions under which the idea of the self is unnecessary. Suppose we are confronted with a person who seems to have both property P and property non-P. Suppose we attempt to resolve this contradiction by saying "He has P in one respect and non-P in another." Now if we can specify the two "respects," there is no need for us to frame the idea of the self at all, for there is then no longer a contradiction to be transferred from the person to the self. Since the person himself is the locus of the saving distinction, the self has no role to play. It is clear, furthermore, that whenever we can specify the relevant "respects" of a person, we do so. We naturally do everything we can to avoid a contradiction.

Yet it is not always possible to specify the relevant "respects." All that I may be able to say is just that Jones has in one respect decided to go but in another respect not decided. But if this is all that I can say, I have not really resolved the contradiction. I have only hedged. I have, in effect, transferred the onus of the contradiction from the person to the unspecified "respects." And reference to such "respects" is tantamount to the idea of the self; for we frame the idea only in order to account for the contradiction in such a way as to show that it need not be ascribed to the person.

"X is in one respect P and in another non-P" does not escape being a contradiction unless we can in principle name the "respects." With physical things, the presumption is that we always can. With persons, we sometimes cannot. This is why selves are associated with persons but not with things. But our first reaction is always to treat the person as a thing, and to suppose that by naming relevant respects we could abolish any apparent contradiction in the person.

The cases in which the idea of the self arises are those in which it is impossible to specify the respect in which the person has a certain property or the respect in which he lacks it. Now if it is in principle impossible to specify these respects, this can only be because they do not exist at all. We suppose that the person is simple in the sense that whatever distinctions must be made refer to the self rather than to the person. When we assert, for example, that Jones has decided to go and has not decided, and at the same time refuse to distinguish one respect of the person Jones in which he has decided to go from another respect in which he has not decided, the implication is that we think that the person as a whole has both decided and not decided, and that there is no respect in which the person who has decided can be distinguished from the person who has not decided. One and the same Jones, simple and indivisible, is the person we have in mind. He is *in toto* qualified as not deciding to go and *in toto* qualified as deciding to go. Now nothing simple could be inconsistent. For whatever is inconsistent must have at least two distinguishable elements: a property P and a property non-P. Hence if a person is simple, then any inconsistency that seems to belong to him must really belong to something complex. It is the self that fulfills this condition. It thus becomes the locus of the contradiction.

Why do I make the paradoxical assertion that the self is the locus of a *contradiction*, rather than taking the apparently safer view that the self is the locus of a *saving distinction* in terms of which a contradiction can be resolved? My discussion of tension is already one answer to this question. In order to answer it again, in a different way, let us suppose that we have said of a person "In one respect he is P and in another respect non-P," and that we are unable to specify these respects. This means that we regard the person as simple. We accordingly frame the idea of the person's self. But if we think of his self as merely the locus of a saving distinction, we have not yet accomplished our purpose. If we suppose, for example, that it is a true self that has P and a false self that has non-P, then all that we have in mind is *the person* has P with respect to a true self and has non-P with respect to a false self. But in this case we have not succeeded in treating the person as simple. He, rather than his self, is the locus of the distinction between the two respects. In order to maintain the simplicity of the person we must transfer from him to something else not only the distinction we have made in order to avoid a contradiction, but also the contradiction itself. That to which we must transfer the contradiction is the person's self.

The idea that there can be something genuinely contradictory about a person is not as unfamiliar as it may seem. Preachers tell us that we are living in contradiction. The life of the sinner is a life shot through with contradictions. We are urged to repent, that is, to acknowledge the contradictory condition of our life. But instead of thus rising to selfhood, we constantly evade the truth.

The evasion takes the form of sophistry and hypocrisy; it is an attempt to escape into a saving distinction that will obviate the need for selfhood. What the preacher is saying is familiar to philosophers of many persuasions. It has often been argued that the world of ordinary .experience is riddled with contradictions—it is a Veil of Maya. Unlike the preacher, however, the philosopher is usually looking for a saving distinction—a Reality in which all the inconsistent features of appearance have a legitimate place.

There are not only selves but also pseudoselves. A pseudoself arises from a pseudocontradiction, that is, one that can be resolved once and for all if we make an appropriate distinction. The self that we think we see in Jones is only a pseudoself—an illusion of which we are the victim—if "Jones has decided to go and has not decided" can be resolved by saying that Jones has decided to betake himself physically but to endorse nothing. Even what I took to be my own self can turn out to be a pseudoself, as when what I took to be an unsolved problem turns out to be solvable. This is why I have no privileged access to my own self. The question now arises, How do you know that there are any selves at all? Might not every contradiction be permanently resolvable? This question can be answered decisively. Consider the proposition "There are genuine contradictions." Whoever disagrees with it presupposes at least one genuine contradiction—namely, that between his position and the position expressed by the proposition with which he disagrees. This is, of course, a non-constructive proof—that is, a proof of something's existence not by producing the thing in question, but merely by showing the absurdity of its nonexistence. But constructive proofs for the existence of many of the properties we ascribe to persons are typically lacking. Suppose we wish to prove, for example, that a person can be wise. Whatever example of a wise person we put forward, someone is sure to raise the question whether that particular person was really wise. The fate that faces examples of inconsistent persons is surely no worse than this. If we suppose that people can be wise, all the cavils to the contrary notwithstanding, we ought also to suppose that people can be inconsistent, all the saving distinctions to the contrary notwithstanding.

If persons were not given as inconsistent, there would be no occasion for the evocation of the self; this is what I mean when I assert that the self presupposes the person. Other philosophers have also held that the self presupposes the person, although not necessarily for the same reason. According to Mead, for example, to have a self is to take the attitude of the Generalized Other.[5] But since Mead always thinks of particular others as persons, not selves (this would after all be circular), it follows that the Generalized Other is a person, albeit a schematic one. For Freud, the ego emerges as the result of one's identification with other persons.[6] It is a general tenet of depth psychology, including Freud's psychoanalysis, that the self arises from tensions in the person. For Kierkegaard, the self results from a confrontation with God as a person.[7] For Strawson, the very notion of a Cartesian ego presupposes the logical primitiveness of the person.[8]

Even some of those thinkers who argue that the self, but not the person, is a fundamental concept—thinkers who might be called "egologists"—could be accused of making an implicit appeal to the person in their arguments for the fundamental status of the self. For Descartes, the proposition that a person can doubt that he doubts is inconsistent, and the substantial ego is posited to permit escape from this inconsistency. But were there no persons, it is difficult to see how there could be any doubts. For Kant, an infinite regress breaks out when we consider whether a person can observe himself as an observer, and only the invocation of the transcendental ego can bring this regress to a halt. The ethical theory of Kant is one in which the authentic self arises only as one recognizes that he is living in a world of persons. Husserl's theory of the transcendental ego approaches being a purely egological theory, but the more emphatically he treats the transcendental ego as an underived phenomenological datum, the more plainly it appears that this ego is not a finite self at all. In order to account for the finite self as such, he is driven, in the fifth *Cartesian Meditation*, to assume the existence of persons in the guise of monads.

Having indicated what I mean by saying that the self presupposes the person, I do not need to take much space to explain why I also believe that the person presupposes the self. To whatever we take to be a person we ascribe the possibility of inconsistency. If something could not in principle be characterized by an inconsistency, we would regard it as a thing rather than as a person. Computers can no doubt duplicate and improve upon the processes of

5. *Mind, Self, and Society*, Chicago, University of Chicago Press, 1934, pp. 154ff.
6. *The Ego and the Id*, London, The Hogarth Press, 1962, pp. 18ff.
7. *The Sickness Unto Death*, Princeton, Princeton University Press, 1946, pp. 127ff.
8. *Individuals*, London, Methuen, 1959, Ch. 3.

intellection, sensation, memory, and learning, but they are not persons, because they cannot possibly be involved in inconsistencies.[9] In fact, they are incapable of even seeming to manifest this possibility. Cats, dogs, and idiots can seem to us to be persons because even if they cannot in fact be caught up in inconsistency, they can imitate the possibility of it, at least when they are raised in a human environment. The actual person, however, is haunted by the genuine and inescapable possibility of falling into contradiction. He is haunted by the possibility of a self.

The self exists primarily in the mode of possibility. Rare are the moments when those contradictions occur that give rise to it. When they do, they merely confirm what we already knew about the person; namely, that it is possible for him to contradict himself. To be acquainted with a person at all is to be aware of this possibility. Of course we can be mistaken, but when we come to realize that contradiction is impossible, we cease to call something a person. Suppose some extremely adaptable and agile creatures should descend from a flying saucer, able to ask questions and give commands in our language. We might be initially inclined to regard them as persons. But if none of them ever exhibited behavior that we could characterize as self-evasive, indecisive, dishonest, corrupt, selfish, vain, or stubborn, we would soon conclude that the creatures were not persons after all but robots taking part in a space probe from another planet. The qualities I have listed are all manifestations of the grasp of a contradiction; and none of them could possibly characterize anything other than a person. A machine, for example, cannot be indecisive. Faced with a problem beyond its competence, it can try to solve it first in one way and then in another, and so back to the first, but it cannot try to solve the problem in both ways at once. Again, a machine can persist in behaving in a certain way even when it has instructions to behave in another way. But such behavior is just a malfunctioning, not stubbornness. It is not stubbornness, because in order to be stubborn we must persist in behaving in a certain way *even though we know that it is the wrong way.* This

9. J. R. Lucas considers the possibility of an inconsistent machine ("Minds, Machines, and Gödel," reprinted in Anderson, *Minds and Machines,* Englewood Cliffs, Prentice-Hall, 1964, pp. 52–3). A machine can no doubt be construed so as to assert that every well-formed formula is a theorem and, as I remarked in Chapter 1, it can be programmed to produce the output "*p* and not-*p.*" But as a physical object, it cannot be in two inconsistent states at once, as can a person. In a somewhat more elaborate form, this was just the point I tried to make in the last chapter.

qualification is essential, because if we try to identify stubbornness as just *persistence* in the wrong, we cannot distinguish it from mere incompetence, a quality that man can share with the machine.

One implication of the last paragraph is that contradictions of many kinds can evoke the self and hence can characterize the person. Indeed, this point must be insisted upon. Not everyone shares Jones's contradiction, and Jones does not share everyone else's. Nor is Jones the only one with a self. Yet not all contradictions are relevant to selfhood. Earlier in this chapter, I made the distinction between selves and pseudoselves. Pseudoselves arise from pseudocontradictions; that is, ones that can be resolved by means of an appropriate distinction. What, if anything, can be said of the class of genuine contradictions—the ones that evoke genuine selves?

Before attempting to answer this question I want to consider what the question presupposes, and how from a certain point of view this very presupposition would be dismissed as patently false. The question presupposes that there is a difference among contradictions: some give rise to the self and others do not. (Both the objection to this presupposition and my reply to the objection are somewhat technical; but the reader without the necessary background in logical theory would probably be unaware of any difficulty in the idea of a multiplicity of different contradictions, and thus could skip, without loss of continuity, to the bottom of p. 28.) Among contradictions giving rise to the self, furthermore, I have already said that there was a difference: there is Jones's indecisiveness, Brown's self-evasiveness and someone else's stubbornness. But it may be objected that all these differences are specious, since all contradictions are in fact equivalent. Is this not indeed a platitude of classical two-valued logic?

The platitude, however, considers contradictions only from an extensional point of view. They are equivalent in that they all have the truth-value *falsum* for every assignment of truth-values to their atomic constituents; they all reduce to the same countertautology. But this does not mean that they are intensionally equivalent. As Lewis has made it possible for us to say, even though contradictions all have the same holophrastic intension, they do not necessarily have the same analytic meaning.[10] There is obviously a distinction in meaning between "Brown is self-evasive," "Brown is stubborn," and "Brown is intelligent and not intelligent"—a distinction that is

10. C. I. Lewis, *An Analysis of Knowledge and Valuation*, pp. 85ff.

obliterated if we reduce all three statements to a simple *falsum*. We deal with self-evasive and stubborn people differently. It is true that we sometimes interpret stubbornness as a form or a manifestation of self-evasiveness, but such an interpretation is not simply an identification of the two concepts. Each of these concepts, furthermore, is different from that of being intelligent and not intelligent, at least in the context of this chapter. When they are applied to a person, they prepare us to deal with the person, but when the phrase "intelligent and not intelligent" is applied to a person it prepares us to make a distinction.

The position might be taken that even if contradictions are different in analytic meaning, they are all alike in that any contradiction implies any proposition whatsoever. This position, too, expresses a platitude of two-valued logic. From this platitude it would follow that if Jones decided and did not decide, then the moon is made of green cheese and pigs have wings, and if Brown is stubborn (and if his stubborn behavior is really inconsistent), time will end on Tuesday. Such implications are embarrassing, to say the least. But I see no reason why we are forced to accept them. The two-valued logic that includes the platitude that a contradiction implies everything has no final claim on our loyalty. Just as the Intuitionists refused to accept the platitude of the excluded middle, and reconstructed logic in such a way that this platitude was no longer true, so we are free to reconstruct logic in such a way that it is no longer the case that a contradiction implies everything. Indeed, there are independent reasons for taking such a step. In their paper "Tautological Entailments,"[11] Anderson and Belnap argue that the platitude in question is in fact no more than a license to commit "truth-functional fallacies of relevance." From the premise $A \ \& \sim A$, either A or $\sim A$ may be relevantly drawn as a conclusion, but not B in general. Anderson and Belnap go on to formulate a criterion that enables us to avoid such fallacies of relevance when we are arguing from a premise of the form $p \ \& \sim p$. Theirs is accordingly a logic without the dubious platitude in question.

I return to the question, "What contradictions invoke the self?" At the moment I can do no more than to answer this question dogmatically, in the hope that examples and discussions scheduled for later in the book will serve as arguments to buttress my answer. What I shall say, then, is that the contradictions that evoke a genuine self

11. *Philosophical Studies*, Vol. 13, 1962, pp. 9–24.

rather than a pseudoself are those rooted in the unity of the person. I tried to show in Chapter 1 how this unity was sufficient to bring into juxtaposition the elements of the contradiction of knowing the right and doing the wrong—indeed, the contradiction implicit in any genuine act of self-reference. In the example of the present chapter, the unity of Jones as a person is sufficient to bar any saving distinction from dissolving the contradiction of his deciding and not deciding.

The appearance of a genuine self not only presupposes the unity of the person, but puts this unity itself in a new perspective. I cannot forbear to mention once more the bewitching Zerlina, who has anyhow already obtruded herself into this chapter. Her "Vorrei e non vorrei" is a contradiction that is unified through the evocation of her self. In the process, furthermore, she becomes for the first time fully human, leaving behind once and for all her life as a carefree peasant girl. Her self, in unifying the contradiction, both confirms her unity as a person and stamps her with this unity. Nor is she the only character in the opera who undergoes this enhancement. There is an implied "Vorrei e non vorrei" in the conduct of the others as well. And they are ennobled by accepting the contradiction.

3 · SELF-, -SELF, AND SELF

Man is spirit. But what is spirit? Spirit is the self. But what is the self? The self is a relation which relates itself to its own self . . . [It] is not the relation but consists in the fact that the relation relates itself to its own self.—Kierkegaard

It might be objected that what I have written in Chapter 2 is one big solecism—a solecism, furthermore, which I could have avoided had I taken seriously warnings already in existence before I wrote the chapter. One such warning is provided by Bernard Mayo in *The Logic of Personality*:

> There is no precedent for the use of the word "self" as an independent noun, capable of being the subject of a verb. The proper use of the expression is not as a word at all, but as a suffix. It is a suffix attached to a personal pronoun which is the subject of a verb. . . The symbol "–self" occurs properly as a suffix to a term in the accusative or other non-nominative case. . . My self is nonsense. . . .[1]

I believe that Mayo's linguistic intuitions are largely to be trusted. Most attempts to use "self" as a substantive can be readily translated into more felicitous language in which the word no longer occurs. Thus if someone were to say "My self went to town" or "My self is enjoying this book," it is obvious that "I" should be substituted for "my self." "I promised my self to do it," if it means anything, means "I promised myself to do it," where "myself" is not a substantive but an indication of reflexivity: Johnstone promised Johnstone to do it. Certainly the identical use of "myself" in "I examined myself to see if there were any broken bones" makes no reference to a self. But a self to which promises could be made is not any more plausible than one that could have broken bones.

1. London, Jonathan Cape, 1952, pp. 93–4.

To suppose that the "myself" in "I promised myself to do it" denotes a self is to commit an error closely similar to the error in supposing that the "nobody" in "I saw nobody on the road" denotes a person. This is a logical error; it arises from a failure to perceive that the logical structure of "I saw nobody on the road" is "Whatever x may be, if x is a person, then I did not see x on the road"—a sentence which carries no reference to "nobody." Similarly, the logical structure of "I promised myself to do it" is "Johnstone promised Johnstone to do it," which does not mention a self. Anyone who thought that the correctness of saying "I promised myself to do it" was a justification for using "self" as a substantive would be committing a solecism on the order of supposing that "nobody" denotes a person.

In the quoted passage, Mayo is concerned with "-self" as a suffix. But similar considerations would apply to the prefix "self-" occurring in such words as "self-control," "self-consciousness," "selfish," "self-destruction," "self-knowledge," and "self-deception." All these expressions have a legitimate use in ordinary language without presupposing the existence of a self, even though, as we shall see, some of them make an oblique reference to the self. If Smith has self-control, Smith is in control of Smith rather than being in control of Smith's self; if Smith has self-esteem, Smith esteems Smith; he does not esteem Smith's self. Self-consciousness, furthermore, is not consciousness of a self; it is either a person's consciousness of himself or consciousness of consciousness. Selfish behavior is no more than the behavior of a person who tends to an abnormal extent to appropriate objects of value and to deny them to others. Since a person can be utterly unaware that he is behaving in this way, it can hardly be maintained that he is acting on behalf of his self. And so on down the list.

Reflections of this kind suggest the enormity of the logical or grammatical mistake of which I might be accused. It is not the mere fact that I have made a mistake that would be regarded as serious; any uneducated person could make that sort of mistake. What is really serious is that I have inflated the mistake into a doctrine, the doctrine that the self exists.

In replying I would begin by characterizing the history of philosophy as a series of solecisms. The difference between the solecisms committed by those philosophers of the past to whom we still pay attention, and those committed by others, is that in the case of the former there have been extenuating circumstances. My own plea, in the case of my use of the word "self," will primarily be that there are circumstances that extenuate this use.

First, though, let me point out that the charge itself is based upon somewhat of a misconception. In fact, it is not always a solecism to use "self" as an independent noun. It was perhaps a solecism when Locke used it in the seventeenth century,[2] but when, over the course of three hundred years, a usage becomes absorbed into ordinary language, it is pointless to continue characterizing it as a solecism. And clearly this usage has been absorbed. Anyone cultivating an eye for occurrences of "self" as a noun can collect a large number of examples in a brief time. The following examples are from my own collection.

2. AGES OF APPLICANTS
    SELF_____
    WIFE_____

Brown is his old self again today.

There, when new wonders ceased to float before,
And thoughts of self came on, how crude and sore
The journey homeward to habitual self!
Keats, "Endymion," Bk. II

His later forsaking of mathematical for political science, and his formidable success in that department, was to be explained by the utter eradication of his earlier self.
John Barth, Giles Goat Boy, p. 547

What ails the frustrated? It is the consciousness of an irremediably blemished self.
Eric Hoffer, The True Believer, p. 58

Such writings as personal letters and diaries, such literary forms as lyric poetry, often "express" the very self of the writer.
Alexander Sesonske, "Saying, Being, and Freedom of Speech," Philosophy and Rhetoric, Vol. I, 1968, p. 31

2. See *An Essay Concerning Human Understanding*, Bk. II, Ch. XXVII. According to the *Oxford English Dictionary (O.E.D.)*, Locke was not the first to use "self" in this way.

For many other examples, see the *O.E.D.* under "Self, C, sb."

I think, furthermore, that there is no mystery about what "self" means in each of these passages: the word refers either to a person, or to the essence of a person (as in the Sesonske quotation), or to a person's conception of himself. In the latter sense the word has currency in contemporary social psychology. In *The Antecedents of Self-Esteem*, for example, Coopersmith says "As defined here, 'the self' is an abstraction that an individual develops about the attitudes, capacities, objects, and activities which he possesses and pursues."[3] It would be odd if we were to dismiss Coopersmith's use of "self" as a solecism. A closely related usage occurs in depth psychology. For Jung, the self is a person's symbolization of himself. It is pointed out that the self

> is not a theoretical construct, as in some present-day psychologies, rationally conceived and reasoned out. . . It has been discovered entirely by . . . empirical methods of observation and classification. . . They are . . . quite different from those of psychoanalysis, whose "censor" and "superego" are perfectly justifiable theoretical designations of categories of events observed during the course of our analysis but are not seen portrayed as such in the psyche's own symbolic self-representation.[4]

The last quotation should remind us that in depth psychology some investigators use "self" as others use "ego"; that is, to denote a theoretical concept. This is the case, for example, in the writings of Harry Stack Sullivan.[5] Of course this use of "self" belongs to technical language, and someone taking Mayo's position might object to my citing this use in my defense, since what I am being accused of is violating the grammar of ordinary language, not misusing technical language. However, our ordinary language is obviously influenced by technical language. The sentence "His ego was deflated" makes ordinary use of a term that presumably was once purely technical. "She was looking for her real self" is psychiatric talk imported into common speech, and as such exemplifies a use in ordinary language of "self" as an independent noun.

3. Stanley Coopersmith, *The Antecedents of Self-Esteem,* San Francisco, W. H. Freeman and Co., 1967, p. 20.
4. J. W. Perry, *The Self in Psychotic Process,* Berkeley, University of California Press, 1953, p. 7.
5. See, for example, *The Interpersonal Theory of Psychiatry,* New York, Norton, 1953, p. 167, Footnote 2. For a discussion of cases in which the two terms are interchangeable, see Muzafer Sherif's article "Self Concept" in *International Encyclopedia of Social Sciences,* New York, Crowell Collier and Macmillan, 1968.

Yet even though ordinary language is not quite as pure as Mayo makes it out to be, I do not wish to argue, as many industrialists do in an analogous situation, that since everybody else pollutes it, it is unfair to forbid me to do so. My argument is rather that it is *more* necessary for me to use the word "self" as an independent noun than it is for the others whose similar usage is forgiven—there are extenuating circumstances that apply to me but not to the others. In order to develop this point, let me remark that these others do use the word "self" somewhat gratuitously. In calling the person, or his conception of himself, or his symbolization of himself, or the essence of person "a self," they are not making full use of the reflexivity built into the affixes "self-" and "-self." If a person conceives or symbolizes himself, the conceiving or symbolizing is, to be sure, a reflexive relation the person bears to himself, but there is nothing essentially reflexive about the concept or the symbolization that is supposed to be the result of the person's bearing such a reflexive relation to himself. Some other word without reflexive force, "ego" for example, would serve just as conveniently as "self" to denote this result.

So far I have considered two ranges of application of the word "self"—ordinary language and the technical language of the sociologists and psychologists. The question of justifying usages falling within these ranges does not really arise at all; ordinary language is simply the linguistic resource that we have to work with, and technical language is arbitrary. Of course, as I have already suggested, it is difficult to make a clear-cut distinction between ordinary and technical language, and there is an interval in which both of these reasons for not raising the question of justification are operative. That the question of justification does arise, however, with respect to the usage of "self" that I am proposing to adopt, is suggested by my promise to appeal to "extenuating circumstances," and by what I have just said about the usefulness of capitalizing on the reflexive force of the affixes "self-" and "-self." It follows that the usage I propose falls within a third range of application of the word—a range that belongs neither to ordinary nor to technical language. (It does, however, blend into technical language, just as the latter does into ordinary language.) This range is philosophical. Philosophical uses occur in a context of justification, and that in two ways. In the first place, the question of the propriety of using the word "self" to refer to the topic under discussion does arise. In the second place, supposing that the propriety of using the word has been established, it remains to be considered whether the self exists; and reasons must be provided for adopting whatever option is adopted. The problems, then, are (1) to justify the use of the word "self" in philosophy, and (2) to justify some thesis expressed by using this word philosophically.

I am now concerned only with (1). I have already indicated along what lines I will seek the required justification. The word "self" is appropriate because there is something essentially reflexive about what it refers to. In fact, nearly every time philosophers have used the word in its philosophical range they have done so as the result of an at least implicit recognition of the reflexivity of what they were talking about. The self has variously been defined as subject, role, agent, locus of freedom, locus of transcendence, locus of identity, spiritual substance, thread of memory, and the like. Only to the extent that these are reflexive ideas can the self be distinguished from the soul. Thus the soul receives impressions from the external world; only to the extent that it can be conscious of itself does it function as a subject. Subject emerged in modern philosophy as the idea that a person has of himself. Similarly, freedom bespeaks a self rather than a soul only when it is seen as autonomy or self-determination; if freedom is indeterminacy, it is sufficient to posit a soul as its locus. Spiritual substance is self only when reflective and thus reflexive.

Role is an essentially reflexive notion, for an individual can have a role only if he is aware of having it; otherwise he merely exercises a function. Mead's analysis of self as in terms of the ideal of the Generalized Other takes this reflexivity into account: one has a self only as far as one controls oneself through this ideal. Agency again implies self-control. The identity realized through the self is self-identity; that is, a person's identification of himself. If all that we are interested in is a person's absolute identity— his identification by God—it is sufficient to speak of his soul as the locus of this identity.

The "self" that Bergson identified with the thread of memory was really a soul rather than a self, because Bergson refused to allow that our reflections on ourselves could be genuinely reflexive. He held that the memories of a past state are assimilated into that state, so that there is never a veridical act of reflection; one cannot reflect on anything without changing it. The vital center into which we are increasingly drawn as we attempt to contemplate ourselves is the soul; and as we are drawn into it, we leave behind subjectivity, self-determination, and self-control.

Man's self is held to be the locus of his transcendence of the world; it is that by virtue of which he can position himself over against the objects of which he is conscious. This transcendence, however, presupposes at least the possibility of a reflexive consciousness of consciousness itself. An alleged state of consciousness that one could never be conscious of being in would not be a state of consciousness at all; it would simply be a nontranscendent absorption into the world.

In the last analysis, I would not regard my enterprise in this book as totally blocked if I were denied the use of the word "self." I would then simply use the word "fles" to denote what I am now using "self" to denote. But if I can show that my own use of "self" is one that refers to an essentially reflexive situation, I can then argue that there is a precedent for my use, and this argument will complete my appeal to extenuating circumstances. I will begin by pointing out the obvious fact that most reflexive relations[6] have nothing to do with the self. Any number is less than or equal to itself; any set is included in itself; a machine can turn off another machine or turn itself off; a computer can program itself. None of these situations presupposes a self. A person, furthermore, can bear many reflexive relations to himself that have nothing to do with a self. Let A be a person and R a relation. Then ARA can readily be exemplified where R assumes such values as "shines the shoes of," "teaches French to," "owns the home of," "carries out plans formulated by," "kills," "employs," and "satisfies." All of these situations can be adequately described without any reference to a self. Indeed, if someone were to make such a reference it would strike us as extremely odd. It is Peters who carries out his own plans, not Peters's self. Peters's self can no more carry out plans than it can walk or drive a car. Can Peters tell an arresting policeman "I was not driving, officer; my self was."? No more can he tell his wife "I did not carry out those plans that I made, dear; my self did."

None of the reflexive relations I have just surveyed presupposes a self in any way. For this reason it may seem that the concept is altogether otiose. Let us consider, however, the statement that Brown is self-evasive. I want to argue that we can correctly analyze this state-

6. A relation R is reflexive, of course, when for any X and Y one chooses, if X bears R to Y (XRY), then X bears R to itself (XRX).

ment only on the assumption that there are selves. And in this respect, the concept of self-evasiveness differs from those listed in the last paragraph at least. The difference is reflected in the fact that while self-employment, and self-satisfaction, for example, are not self-contradictory concepts, self-evasion *is* self-contradictory. For the latter concept presupposes that one and the same entity both occupies a certain position and retreats from that position. If two entities or more were involved, one retreating from another, we would not use the expression "self-evasion," but would speak instead, perhaps, of "repulsion." Thus we can speak of the mutual repulsion of the atoms of liquid helium in its superfluid state, but no one would say that the liquid manifested self-evasion. It is never proper to apply the latter expression to a physical phenomenon. Let us ask, then, to what phenomena it does apply. I have asserted that "*X* evades *X*" is a contradiction. A contradiction is the simultaneous assertion of two propositions, each of which is the logical contradictory of the other. It is because the occasion for making an assertion of this kind never arises in science that the expression "self-evasion" never applies to a physical phenomenon, or, for that matter, to any phenomenon studied in a science. What, then, is the occasion for asserting both of two contradictory propositions?

I think such an occasion arises only when the unity of a person overrides the consideration that the propositions are contradictory. And in this case the person's self arises as the locus of the contradiction.

What self-evasion could be if there were no particular point of view, no self, from which it could be acknowledged, I do not know. Self-evasion is essentially the activity of a self. This is why the Sartrean conception of an impersonal consciousness essentially describable as self-evasive strikes me as anomalous. In fact, Sartre's critique of Freud in the chapter of *Being and Nothingness* devoted to "Bad Faith" makes very much the point that I have been trying to make in arguing that self-evasion is intrinsically self-contradictory.

> The very essence of the reflexive idea of hiding something from oneself implies the unity of one and the same psychic mechanism and consequently a double activity in the heart of unity, tending on the one hand to maintain and locate the things to be concealed and on the other hand to repress and disguise it.[7]

7. *Being and Nothingness*, tr. Hazel Barnes, New York, Philosophical Library, 1956, p. 53.

By "psychic mechanism" Sartre appears to mean almost or exactly what I mean by "self." But this concept plays no systematic part in Sartre's exposition. Throughout the book, the self is referred to as a fugitive and illusory concept.

The decisive difference, then, between the case of self-evasion and those of self-employment, shining one's shoes, teaching French to oneself, and so on, is that in this case we are concerned with a contradiction. The self becomes relevant when we are confronted not merely with a reflexive relation, but with an inconsistent one. Another way of putting the point is to say that the self arises when an irreflexive relation must inconsistently be treated as reflexive. "Evades" is irreflexive. If X evades Y, then X must differ from Y. Yet Brown's self-evasiveness is a case in which one and the same Brown evades Brown. This is a contradiction, and Brown's self arises as a locus of the contradiction, not as a locus of reflexivity.

The self is evoked, then, not by a reflexive relation as such, and not by a contradiction as such, but by a statement that contradicts itself by attributing reflexivity to an irreflexive relation. But this cannot be the whole story; for any contradiction can be expressed as the attribution of reflexivity to an irreflexive relation, and any irreflexive relation can be the subject of an irresponsible or silly ascription of reflexivity. Thus, for any statement p, instead of "p and not-p" we can always say "The relation *contradicts* holds between p and itself (that is, is reflexive)." (This shows, incidentally, how "Jones decides and does not decide" can be treated in terms of a reflexive relation.) And there are silly statements like "Richardson is greater than himself, stands next to himself, is his own father." There is clearly no part for the self to play in connection with such statements. Statements that do evoke the self are those whose inconsistency stems from the absolute unity of the person—a unity which can survive the reflexive use of some irreflexive relations, but obviously not of all. The inconsistency must be a pragmatic contradiction —one realized through a person's action. It is difficult to think of a better example of such a contradiction than self-evasion, especially as described by Sartre.

Of course, nothing requires the reflexive ascription of irreflexive relations to persons to be accepted at face value even when they are not silly. When I say "Brown is self-evasive" I can be mistaken. There may be a saving distinction which I do not at the moment see, or which I may never see. Nothing guarantees that I know the truth about Brown.

How, precisely, does the self figure in our grasp of a statement inconsistently treating an irreflexive relation as reflexive? It provides a fusion. We might be tempted, for example, to interpret "Brown evades himself" as meaning "$Brown_1$ evades $Brown_2$," where the subscripts denote different elements of Brown. But once Brown's self is introduced, it allows $Brown_1$ to fuse with $Brown_2$. We see that one and the same person is both occupying a position and retreating from it. If it never occurred to us to ascribe a self to Brown, then $Brown_1$ and $Brown_2$ would never fuse, and there would be no contradiction. Perhaps we would then simply treat Brown's body as the seat of several alternating personalities. At the same time, if there were not an implicit contradiction, it would never occur to us to ascribe a self to Brown.

Is there any difference between self-evasion and some other sort of self-contradictory behavior such as self-deception?

Superficially at least, there is a difference between the forms of the contradictions in the two cases, and it may be helpful to exhibit this difference. The contradiction in self-evasion is simply that of retreating from a position while continuing to occupy it. The contradiction in self-deception can be derived as follows: if A deceives B about X, then (1) A knows the truth about X, (2) A tells B a falsehood about X, and (3) B believes what A tells him about X. Hence if A deceives A about X (that is, deceives himself) we have: (1) A knows the truth about X, (2) A tells A a falsehood about X, and (3) A believes what A tells him about X. Now (1) implies that A *believes* the truth about X: he believes some proposition "p," which is the truth about X. But (3) means that A believes "not-p." Hence A believes both p and not-p. This is a contradiction. A number of ways of attempting to avoid the conclusion that it is a contradiction have been considered by Frederick Siegler in his article "Self-Deception."[8] Siegler shows that none of them is satisfactory. He concludes that "*A* deceives himself" is simply a rhetorical device for saying "*How could A* believe such nonsense?" Yet even if we can translate "*A* deceives himself" in this way, the translation is not as innocuous as Siegler seems to think. We would not exclaim "*How could A* believe such nonsense?" if we knew that A could not help believing what he believed. We would not use this expression, for example, in speaking of a member of a primitive tribe who entertained some belief we know to be false. We would not use it in speaking of an idiot.

8. *Australasian Journal of Philosophy and Psychology*, Vol. XLI, 1963, pp. 29–43.

We would use it only of an *A who ought to know better*. Why ought he to know better? The only answer seems to be that he has been exposed to explanations and arguments which, in a person who is not an idiot, produce belief. By hypothesis, however, we do not think that *A* is an idiot. In fact what we really think is that *A* really believes something other than the "nonsense" in question. But he believes the nonsense, too. He accepts a contradiction. The fact that people do use expressions like *"How could A* believe such nonsense?"* is thus further evidence of the ubiquity of contradiction in life.

Whatever the analysis of the particular contradiction involved in self-deception, the self has the same unificatory role that it has in self-evasion: it brings together in a single focus the poles of the contradiction. This is one further case, then, in which the ascription of reflexivity to an irreflexive relation ("Deceives") requires and evokes the self—not because the prefix in "Self-deception" names anything, but because the reflexivity implied by the prefix is in fact contradictory.

A few pages back, I argued that the use of the word "self" in the philosophical range requires justification in two ways. We must justify not only the choice of the word but also the belief that what it denotes exists. On the first point, I have argued that "self" is an appropriate word to denote an aspect of a situation to which reflexivity is ascribed. I turn now to the second point. Many philosophers who have thought of the self as subject, role, agent, locus of freedom, and so on, have supposed that it existed as something that undergirds or underwrites one or another of these functions; or else, because they could find no such psychic substructures in the human makeup, they have denied that it existed. (Hume, for example, based his denial of the self's existence on his failure to find any impressions of his own unity.) My own view, however, is that any such supposition ascribes to the self a misplaced concreteness. The self does not exist as a bearer of subjectivity, a substance, a role, or a locus of freedom or identity—Hume was right, in my view—but to say that it does not exist in any such mode is not to deny that it exists altogether—here Hume leapt to an unwarranted conclusion. It is rather that the self is evoked by the execution of the functions in question. There is, as I shall try to show in succeeding chapters, a contradiction implicit in being a subject, having a role, or acting freely. The self arises as the locus not of subjectivity, role, or freedom, but of the *contradiction* of subjectivity, role, or freedom. How it does this should by now be a familiar story. The relation of the self to self-deception which I have outlined in this chapter could serve as a paradigm. In later chapters I will try to exhibit some of the other relevant contradictions. My efforts, if successful, will show that not only traditional views of the self but also some aspects of the traditional account of the soul result from misplaced concreteness. The soul, for example, has been regarded as an element of man's nature that survives death. What I want to propose as a substitute for this thesis is that the very notion of surviving death is self-contradictory, and that when we bring this contradiction into focus, the self emerges.

My argument presupposes that when a person contemplates his role, memory, or freedom he will in due course properly come upon a contradiction. Nearly every philosopher throughout the history of the discipline has denied this, for nearly every one of them has supposed that the purpose of philosophy as a rational inquiry is to dissipate the contradictions that people stumble into in the course of their reflections. Only mystics, Hegelians, Marxists, and Existentialists have supposed any contradictions ineliminable, and Hegelians and Marxists have regarded them as only provisionally ineliminable. I make this point not in order to draw any comfort from my precursors but just to indicate that since I know that most of my predecessors were not precursors, I realize the enormity of what I am doing.

4 · THE PERSON AND THE FIRST PERSON

What is meant by the word "person" has, in contrast with the ego, something of a totality, which is self-sufficient.—Scheler

I hope I have made it clear what kind of an inference I am proposing to make from the affixes "self-" and "-self" to the existence of the self. I am not in the least arguing that the self is what these affixes name. It would be a mistake, I am sure, to suppose that they name anything. I do not think it is a mistake, however, to feel that on some occasions when the use of these reflexive affixes is appropriate a fusion is accomplished through an agency for which it is convenient to have a name. I might have made up a name, or used a name like "ego," which is in current use in a sense closely allied to what I have in mind. I prefer "self," which is also in current use in a sense closely allied to what I have in mind, because it suggests the reflexivity of the transactions through which that which it denotes is brought into existence.

"Ego" is the Greek and Latin first personal pronoun. There is no more reason to suppose that something arcane is named by the first personal pronoun in any language than there is to suppose that something arcane is named by the reflexive affixes "self-" and "-self." To be sure, names can sometimes be substituted for the first personal pronoun, but what is named thereby is hardly arcane. When I say "I went to town," I mean simply "Johnstone went to town." Of course when Smith says "I went to town," he does not mean "Johnstone went to town"; the possibility of making a substitution in one case does not mean we have found a name equivalent to "I." There is, as we shall see, no name equivalent to "I."

My point can be summarized by saying that "I" is primarily an autobiographical word, not an egological one. Even the most intimate secrets that I can express by using "I" are only Johnstone's secrets; that is, they pertain to a person but not to a self. The question "Who am I?" asked by a victim of amnesia is not, to be sure, autobiographical, but it is not egological either. It means simply "The person standing before you requires identification." When one's identity is not in question, "I" is autobiographical in a way that systematically precludes it from being egological. No matter in how much detail I tell what I am, using "I" to tell it, I cannot hope that the use of "I" will take me a single step toward describing my self.

Another way of making the point that "I" is not a name of the self is to note that while both "I went to town" and "Johnstone went to town" make sense, "My self went to town" does not. Yet I want to argue that the existence of the self is *presupposed* by some uses of the first personal pronoun. It is not, of course, presupposed by *all* uses of this pronoun, any more than it is presupposed by *all* uses of the affixes "self-" and "-self." A computer programmed to prove theorems might well be instructed in certain cases to return the message "I am at the end of my resources. I cannot find any proof of this theorem." No one would want to contend that because the computer used the word "I" in a very natural way, it showed that it possessed a self. My view, however, is that there are cases in which the use of "I" does imply possession of a self. One of my tasks in this chapter is to distinguish these cases from the others.

The most penetrating inquiry that I know of into the function and implications of our use of the first personal pronoun is to be found in S. Coval's recent book *Scepticism and the First Person*.[1] While brief, this book is complex. My purposes will be served by examining just one of its themes. Coval argues that while there is a difference between the first personal pronoun and the others, it is a merely contingent difference and not one that warrants any kind of skepticism. The difference he recognizes is that "although all pronouns may be voiced by any particular speaker, 'I' occurs in his mouth unlike 'you' or 'he' " (p. 1). There is, in other words, something peculiar about a speaker's use of "I." Anyone may say "Jones is cold" but only Jones may say (of himself) "I am cold." It has seemed natural to transfer the peculiarity of "I" to some of the predicates used in sentences containing "I." It has been assumed, for example, that paralleling the difference between "I" and "Jones"

1. London, Methuen, 1966. I shall refer to passages in this book by means of page numbers in parentheses.

there is a difference between two meanings of "cold," for if only Jones can say of himself "I am cold" it seems plausible to infer that what Jones means when he says "I am cold" is not what anyone else means in saying of Jones "He is cold."

It is precisely here that the worm of skepticism has seemed to show its ugly head. For, as Coval puts the matter, "Since there is but a single list of epithets which seem to connect to all pronouns without prejudice, the . . . difference [between "I" in Jones's mouth and "he" in mine] will seem to introduce a double life into this list. Well-known skeptical problems ensue when such double life is granted the predicates of personal pronouns" (p. 1). The skeptical problems Coval has in mind could take as their paradigm the problem of understanding Jones's statement "I am cold."

One way in which Coval deals with this issue is by claiming that the asymmetry between Jones's "I" and my "he" is merely contingent. While linguistic economies are effected by the use of the pronoun "I," other devices are available which, while not so economical, perform the function of "I" without manifesting its asymmetry. Hence even if asymmetry does imply doubts, the latter are not necessary, and hence cannot properly be erected into a doctrine of skepticism.

The function of the pronoun "I," in Coval's view, is simply to facilitate self-reference.[2] It is merely a device by which a person makes it clear that he is referring to himself rather than to anyone else. Certainly this is its most important function. The victim of amnesia whom I mentioned earlier is simply using the "I" of "Who am I?" to refer to himself. But minor reservations are possible. When a person on the other side of the door is asked "Who is there?" he may reply "I" (or "me"), thus not *referring* to himself, but *identifying* himself by the sound of his voice. Such cases, however, do not seem to produce the asymmetry that is produced when "I" is used to achieve self-reference. Coval accordingly asks whether other devices of self-reference are possible which do not produce asymmetry. He exhibits three. One is "a convention of speaker-restricted 'names'" (p. 23). Since by hypothesis there will have

---

2. Notice that self-reference in this sense is not the same as the self-reference which propositions are sometimes regarded as exhibiting and which is sometimes held to be the source of logical antinomies. A proposition that refers to X is *about X;* if it refers to itself, it is about itself. It is nonsense, however, to say that a person who refers to X is about X. When a person refers, he performs an act; when a proposition refers, it does not.

to be particular conventions permitting us to identify speaker-restricted names *as* speaker-restricted, there is "no formally general way of indicating the difference between such speaker-restricted and non-speaker-restricted 'names' " (p. 23). Coval gives no examples of conventions of the sort he has in mind. One example might be the convention of adding "-self" to a name to indicate that it is speaker-restricted. Thus "Johnstoneself" might be a name that only I am permitted to use of myself. In this case there is no one word that everyone can use to refer to himself. The "economy and generality of our first person device" is lost, even though unique self-reference is attained.

Another device is the use of proper names as they are used now and without benefit of speaker-restricted names. This device is more economical than the former in that it does not require two sets of names, one speaker-restricted and one other-restricted. In a society committed to the use of this device, however, in order for a speaker to make clear that he was using his own name, he would have to do something like pointing to himself when using it, and this extra activity would represent a loss of economy.

A third possible device for achieving self-reference is to use "this" instead of "I." Unlike the names proposed before, "this" is a single word that everyone in turn can use to refer to himself. But a speaker can also use it of others than himself. Pointing, or some such device, will once again have to be introduced so that the needed distinctions can be made; we have still failed to achieve the economy of "I."

It is not only the economy of the first personal pronoun that disappears when we resort to devices such as those enumerated. Its asymmetry also vanishes, according to Coval. The skeptical problem presupposes a difference between what I mean when I use "I" to refer to myself alone and what others mean when they use "I" to refer to themselves alone. But no such difference stigmatizes the devices mentioned. Whether names are speaker-restricted or not, no one except me could use my name to refer to himself, so that the question does not arise whether my name as used by another to refer to himself means the same as my name as used by me to refer to myself. The remaining device, the word "this," *can* be used by another to refer to himself as well as by me to refer to myself, but it cannot be used by me to refer to myself *alone* or by another to refer to himself *alone;* so once again there is no asymmetry. We could, of course, require users of a self-referential "this" to point to themselves. Here, I think, there would be an asymmetry; what I mean by saying "This is cold" while pointing to myself is not what Jones means by "This is cold" while pointing to himself. But Coval surely does not mean to argue that "I" is the only asymmetrical self-referential device; it is sufficient to show that self-reference is sometimes attainable without asymmetry.

Coval summarizes the function of the first personal pronoun by calling it "a device of performatory reference." The adjective "performatory" stems, of course, from Austin's theory of performative utterances. The issuing of such an utterance, according to Austin, "is the performing of an action—it is not normally thought of as just saying something."[3] Thus to say "I promise to go" is more than just to say something; it is to make a promise. Similarly, "Our conventions are such that to utter 'I . . .' is to refer, by way of that act of utterance itself and its necessary connection to the speaker, to the speaker himself" (Coval, p. 36).

It is at some place as this that I think issue might be joined with Coval, for he writes of speakers and also of self-referrers (p. 56). He seems to assume that their existence raises no question. They belong to an ontology of unquestioned entities that lies at the horizon of Coval's discussion. I want to show, however, that speakers and self-referrers do not escape the paradoxes to which users of the first personal pronoun are subject.

Self-reference, whether accomplished through a speaker-restricted name, through pointing to oneself, or through the first personal pronoun, is an achievement that Coval takes for granted, but it may in fact be more difficult than he imagines. Let me begin with pointing to oneself. Mechanical devices can point; a compass points to the north magnetic pole. Can such a device point to itself? If a compass had a long flexible needle and if a piece of magnetized iron were embedded in the compass, the needle could double back and point toward the compass. But it would not be pointing *at* the compass; it would only be pointing *at* the iron. Even if we did not know *what* the needle was pointing at, we would never say that the compass was pointing at itself. It could at best only be pointing at *part* of itself. To achieve self-reference, however, is to point at oneself *as a totality*. The needle must point at the compass *including itself*.

3. J. L. Austin, *How to DO Things with Words*, Oxford, Oxford University Press, 1962, pp. 6–7.

But there is no mechanical model for an indicator pointing at itself. Even if we bend a needle into a full circle, so that the head is pointing at the tail, the needle cannot be construed as pointing at itself. Somewhere we must introduce a distinction between the part of the needle that does the pointing and the part that is pointed at, for the very act of pointing presupposes a difference between what does the pointing and what is pointed at. If we do not introduce such a distinction, we are caught in a contradiction, because we are asserting that there is only one part while presupposing that there are two. We may accordingly be driven into an infinite regress. In order to avoid the outright contradiction of supposing that a looped needle can point at itself as a totality, we can perhaps think of a needle which points at a needle which points at a needle . . . , but we cannot envisage the series as a totality.

I jump from the pointing behavior of mechanical devices to that of humans because I am not sure whether there is any animal except man which can point at itself as a totality. Any such animal would have to be able to conceive of itself as a totality, but this seems to me a difficult feat, akin perhaps to that of recognizing one's own image in the mirror. If there are such animals, I have no objection to applying to them what I want to say about humans. Self-reference by pointing is still a difficult feat. In fact, it is not even quite as easy for a *human* to achieve as Coval seems to think. If one tries to refer to oneself by pointing at oneself, the act is often at least ambiguous. If someone says "This is cold" and points at himself, his hearers will likely take him to mean that the part of his body he is pointing at is cold. Fortunately, there is a way in which humans can avoid this ambiguity. One can say "This person is cold" while pointing at oneself and what is pointed at will then come into focus as the entire person, including the pointing finger. It is as if the person were standing outside himself pointing at himself. We may not regard this as an outright contradiction, but if we think about it we can find it a troublesome situation to contemplate.

What is peculiar to a person is his capacity to refer to himself as a totality. A machine cannot refer to itself as a totality. It might be supposed that we could build a machine that would point at itself and say "This machine is operating at 3600 r.p.m." A moment's reflection, however, will suffice to reveal the phenomenology of this arrangement. The arrangement would break down into a machine operating at 3600 r.p.m. and a tachometer feeding into a tape recorder. The tachometer could not be taken to be including itself in the totality it was characterizing. We would automatically take the phrase "this machine" to refer to a system apart from the tachometer.

Imagine a robot in the shape of a person pointing at itself and saying "This person's pulse rate is 78." If we refused to be taken in by its claim to be a person, we would once again see other-reference rather than self-reference. We would see a pulse counter commenting on a totality in which it was not itself included.

A person, however, can refer to himself by pointing at himself and saying "This person's pulse rate is 78." In this case it would be at least a curious distortion of the way in which we usually regard persons, to distinguish a pulse counter from the rest. It is the *person* who both has the pulse and counts it.

The difference between the last two cases is the difference between a false and a true ascription of "person." Persons have a unity that no machine can possibly have—a unity so cohesive that it can absorb a contradiction. (Of this unity I have already spoken in Chapter 1.) This is why the person can self-ascribe a pulse rate while the robot can only other-ascribe it. It remains to be said, however, by virtue of what criterion we call something a person and refuse to call something else one. The criterion cannot be that of *behaving* like a person, since the robot can do that as well as the real person. I have already suggested what I think the criterion is. Only a being that can conceive of itself as a totality can refer to itself. In cases of other-reference, we do not require that the referrer conceive of anything at all; we do not insist, for example, that the compass needle be able to conceive of the north magnetic pole, whatever that could possibly mean. But the reason we refuse to regard the robot's pointing as self-reference is that we know that it cannot conceive of itself as a totality. It cannot conceive of anything at all; it is not even conscious.

One of the propositions central to Coval's exposition is that "there are not two sorts of reference" (p. 41). There is not, he says, "a type-difference between pointing at oneself and pointing specifically elsewhere" (p. 41). "Pointing to oneself," he asserts, "is as different from pointing to another object as pointing to one object is from pointing at another" (p. 42). In the case of the first personal pronoun, there is, of course "an important functional difference between reference and self-reference" (p. 34), but this difference in function (the difference, namely, between the performatory function of the first personal pronoun and the designative function of demonstratives) is not a difference in type. I do not think, however, that Coval succeeds in proving that this is so. His only argument, for example, to the conclusion that pointing to oneself and pointing specifically elsewhere are not different in type seems to be that non-asymmetrical self-reference can be achieved by pointing to oneself. Since by nonasymmetrical self-reference is meant simply self-reference not different in type from other-reference, this argument, if it is an argument, begs the question.

For my part, I have asserted that there is a difference between self-reference and other-reference, but I have yet to establish that the difference is one of type in Coval's sense; that is, that self-reference is necessarily asymmetrical. I turn to that difference now.

A person can refer to himself by pointing to himself only if he can conceive of himself as a totality. This implies that the person must be conscious; it does not, of course, imply that he must be conscious of himself as a totality, whatever that might mean. Thus Jones can say "This person is cold" (or "This person is six feet tall," or "This person is in pain"), pointing to himself, only because he can conceive of himself as a totality. If I say "This person is cold," pointing to Jones, I too must conceive of Jones as a totality—it is *all* of Jones that is cold, not just the part my finger happens to be pointing to. The question remains, however, how I can be sure that my conception of Jones as a totality is the same as Jones's conception of himself as a totality?

Coval is at pains to point out that there is no reason why in principle I cannot verify that Jones is *cold* when he says he is. To do so, I need only duplicate in myself the conditions under which Jones says he is cold. Much more, of course, may be required than merely sitting in the same room with Jones. If his feeling results from poor circulation, then I must induce the same poor circulation in myself. If it is psychosomatic, then I must undergo the same psychic trauma that is responsible for it. I may have to relive Jones's whole life. In some such way it is always in principle possible for me to check another's claims about his states. Coval's point is that there are not inner states as opposed to percepts of outer things. There are always ways that

> are as close as we need get to checking on an utterance of
> another without doing the impossible, that is, without being

him. *But this is a general truth for all classes of utterance whether they are of oneself or of external things, whether of states of consciousness or physical objects.* And if we are satisfied with such possible checks in the case of some physical object statements then we must be satisfied with them in the case of purely personal utterances. (p. 93)

He goes on to say that

Lack of satisfaction with the production of "sufficiently similar circumstances" which fill the epistemological gap between me and you would lead, in consistency, to lack of acceptance not only in the sort of case . . . where mental states are involved but also in the case of *any* ascription involving even material objects; I cannot have the basis of saying that the shoe shines that Enos has for saying this. (p. 99)

I am willing to grant both (a) the outside possibility of being able to verify Jones's statement "This is cold" (uttered while Jones is pointing to himself) and (b) the relatively secure thesis that what Jones *means* by "cold" when he ascribes it to himself is what I mean by it when I ascribe it to him. I think Coval has established, if it needed establishing, that there is no asymmetry affecting the *predicates* that people ascribe to themselves and to one another. The question remains, however, whether my *conception of Jones as a totality* can be the same as Jones's conception of himself as a totality, provided the conditions are the same. What are the relevant conditions? When Jones points to himself, his gesture is exclusive as well as inclusive. He indicates himself, but specifically not me (or you). One of the conditions under which Jones conceives himself as a totality then, is the condition of distinguishing himself from others. Notice that nothing like this condition applies to Jones's feeling of cold. There is nothing in the feeling as such that implies that it *cannot* be shared by others. But Jones cannot conceive of himself as a totality without conceiving of himself in such a way that no one else could share the conception.

The premises on which my argument is based are the following: (1) If w shares x's conception of y, then x ascribes to y all and only those properties that w ascribes to y. (2) If y is a distinct person from x and x is not suffering from delusions,[4] then x ascribes to

4. I am indebted to Professor Mason Myers of Northern Illinois University for pointing out the need for this clause to accommodate the case in which, for example, I identify myself with Napoleon although I am in fact different from Napoleon.

himself the property of being different from y. (3) If w shares x's conception of x, and w ascribes some property to x, then w must ascribe that same property to himself. This last premise makes it clear that one cannot *share* anything with another without possessing it to exactly the extent to which the other possesses it. This point would readily be conceded with respect to the cold that I share with Jones: to share that cold I must possess it too. A principle of parity requires applying the same condition to whatever I ascribe to Jones as I share his conception of himself; I do not really *share* this conception unless I ascribe the same properties to *myself*.

Assuming now that I am different from Jones, that I do not suffer from delusions, and that I share Jones's conception of himself, it can be deduced that I ascribe to myself the property of being different from myself. We can escape this contradiction only by maintaining the asymmetry of Jones's conception of himself.

It is important to be meticulous in our metaphysics; Coval certainly is. Early in his book he considers the claim expressed by saying "My states of consciousness cannot be the states of consciousness of anyone else." He argues that this statement is exactly on a par with statements we could make about certain properties of a material object. One might say, as he does, "The particular colour . . . of this hand is the colour which only this hand may have. Its colour is *its* colour. That it may be duplicated or have kindred exemplifications is beside the point" (p. 16). But in such cases, as Coval points out, "It is an already particular exemplification that we are being asked to other-ascribe" (p. 16). According to the ordinary laws of individuation, of course, "we cannot other-ascribe from one object to another an object's systematically individuating features. We cannot, for instance, other-ascribe its space-time history. But," Coval goes on to say, "it is probably mistaken to feel that any of the object's properties are systematically unique or individual in the way its space-time history may be" (pp. 16–17). Coval cannot see any reason why what he says about impersonal objects would not apply to persons as well. The implication is that since states of consciousness are not systematically individuating, they can be other-ascribed from one person to another, with the trivial exception that a *particular exemplification* of a state of consciousness cannot be other-ascribed. In this connection Coval speaks of "a kind of Leibnitzian illusion, the illusion that because individuals are systematically unique their properties are too" (p. 18).

My own view of the nature of the person is perhaps Leibnitzian, but I do not believe that it is an illusion. I would certainly grant everything I have quoted Coval as having said about the scope and limits of other-ascription. I completely agree that whatever state of consciousness Jones has I may have too under sufficiently similar circumstances. But when Jones refers to himself by pointing to himself, his conception of himself as a totality *is* individuating, because it specifically excludes what is not Jones. Hence it may be ascribed only to Jones. Whether Jones's spacetime history is also individuating is a thorny question; my guess is that if we ever had to assign priorities between it and Jones's conception of himself as a totality, we would assign the higher priority to the latter. Thus if across the behavior of a single body we saw one person's conception of himself as a totality suddenly replaced by another such conception, we would say that one person had replaced another. And if in Singapore there should suddenly appear a person conceiving of himself as a totality in precisely the same way as did poor Jones, who died some time ago in New York, what further evidence in favor of reincarnation could we require?

At this point I do not think there is anything I need to add in order to explain why I feel that when self-reference is accomplished by pointing to oneself it is asymmetrical, in the sense that what Jones means when he points to himself and says "This person is cold" is nothing that I could possibly mean—at least, so far as "this person" is concerned. I turn now to the second way in which Coval says we can accomplish self-reference: specifically, by taking the role of speaker.

Two of the self-referential devices described by Coval presuppose the possibility of a speaker. These are the speaker-restricted name and the first personal pronoun. In attempting to elicit precisely what this possibility is that is presupposed by the two devices, I will have both devices in mind.

In an article called "On the Creation of a Speaker"[5] Arthur Cody points out that there are grave difficulties in understanding what it is to be a speaker. He concludes that it is a miracle that speakers should have come into being at all. My agreement with Cody can be expressed by saying that to my way of thinking it is every bit as hard to refer to oneself by speaking as it is to do so by pointing. Coval, however, does not seem to be aware of any difficulty in the concept of a self-referential speaker.

5. *Mind*, Vol. 77, 1968, pp. 68–76.

Speaking is inherently reflexive. A speaker is always a member of his own audience. He speaks to others only if he speaks to himself, that is, if he understands what he is saying. If he does not speak to himself he is not a speaker but a mere reproducer of speech. Yet there is no mechanical model for the activity of speaking to oneself. One can speak only to what could, in principle, listen. One cannot speak to the wall, for the wall cannot listen. Hence one can speak to oneself only because in principle one could listen to one's own speaking. But no machine could listen to its own speaking. If we were told that a machine could in fact do this, we would immediately assume that there were, in effect, two machines—a speech-reproducing machine and another machine actuated by speech sounds. Only the unity of a person is sufficiently cohesive to permit speaker and listener to merge.

When a speaker explicitly refers to himself, the difficulty is much the same as with the concept of a self-referential pointer. If a machine said "I am cold," we would immediately distinguish the attention-getting part of the machine from the cold part. Even assuming what I would in my less conciliatory moments be inclined to deny, and what Cody would certainly deny—that in getting attention the machine is functioning as a speaker at all—it is still not a self-referential speaker; the part that is doing the speaking cannot be referring to *itself* as the part that is cold.

It might be claimed, however, that there are machines that do call attention to themselves *in toto;* for example, alarm clocks. It seems to me, though, that an alarm clock, rather than referring to itself, refers to the time. Compare the ringing of the alarm clock with the utterance of a person saying "I am cold." The ringing would not properly be translated by any statement beginning with the first personal pronoun; the alarm clock is not saying, for example, "I am seven o'clock." (I will, however, comment shortly on the possibility that it is saying "I am *registering* that it is seven o'clock.") Perhaps, on the other hand, a time bomb is a machine that achieves self-reference by calling attention to itself. But having called attention to itself, it does not go on to say anything *about* itself; the act of self-reference is not completed. The explosion of the time bomb is like the person who simply says "I," not by way of answering a question, but as an opening gambit in a conversation. Such a person has not succeeded in referring to himself.

Perhaps the following counterexample might be offered in the

attempt to show that a machine *could* use the first personal pronoun
to refer to itself. The machine I have in mind is comparable to many
now in existence. Its function is to search for books in a library. If
it finds a requested book, it sends it out to the would-be borrower
by way of a chute. If it does not find the book, it says "I am sorry,
but I am unable to locate the book you have asked for." It might be
supposed that this machine achieves self-reference by speaking.
However, even assuming that the machine can speak at all, it is certainly not referring to *itself* in the act of speaking. It is referring
to the books in the library, or to a certain set of them, and saying
that the book in question is not one of those in the library or set.
That the machine cannot locate the book is not a fact about the
machine at all. Similarly, that the alarm clock registers seven o'clock
is not a fact about the alarm clock—or if it is, it is not a fact about
the *whole* alarm clock, including the bell.

Having suggested some of the difficulties that impede the
attempt to refer to oneself by speaking, I turn now to the question whether such self-reference is asymmetrical. This question can
already be decisively answered in much the way in which we dealt
with the question of whether self-pointing is asymmetrical. For in
order to speak self-referentially, one must speak of oneself as a
totality; there is no distinction between the part of the person that
says "I am cold" and the part that is cold. And a person can speak of
himself as a totality only if he has some conception of himself as
a totality. But for purely formal reasons, my conception of another
person as a totality can never be the same as his conception. However, Coval provides an additional handhold upon the problem, and
we might as well use that, too. He says, "Speech is action, and, if it
needs adding, intentional action" (p. 73). The question might arise
"How can I share in Jones's action in saying 'I am cold'?" Coval
makes it quite clear that this question rests upon a metaphysical mistake: "Actions are non-transferable because they get their identity
from the spatiotemporal body of which they are modes. In order
for them to be transferable the possessing particulars themselves
would have to be so; that is, they would have to be non-particulars
or non-identities" (p. 42). What happens, however, if we press the
question further and ask "How can I share in Jones's *intention* in
saying 'I am cold'?" Intentions do not, at least in any obvious way,
get their identity from any spatiotemporal body of which they are
modes; even though Jones's *action* is identifiable only in terms of

Jones, Jones's *intention* must have an identity apart from Jones; if we could not ascribe the same intention to two different persons it is difficult to see what could be meant by calling it an intention in the first place. Of course Coval can claim to be talking about intention in the sense in which Jones's intention *does* get its identity from the spatiotemporal body of which it is a mode, and he can then use the same argument that he did in connection with a person's action. The fact remains, however, that we need another sense of "intention" in which intentions *are* transferable. Hence Coval must sooner or later face the question "How can I share Jones's intention in saying 'I am cold'?" The only answer, furthermore, for which he has prepared us is of the form "Under sufficiently similar circumstances I will have the same intentions." But this is an extremely odd statement. It suggests that intentions arise under conditions. Feelings and sensations do arise under conditions; this is how the cold that I feel can be exactly the cold that Jones feels. But suppose that an action is such that we want to say "Given sufficiently similar conditions, a similar action will occur." I think we would be disinclined to say that the action was intentional at all. It is instead a kind of reflex. Of course, there are *necessary* conditions that must prevail in order for Jones and me both to say truly "I am cold." But if we think of those conditions as sufficient, as they are in the case of Jones and me *feeling* cold, then whenever the conditions are met Jones and I will both *say* "I am cold." But clearly our saying "I am cold" under such conditions loses its intentional status. It is intentional only if I can choose *not* to say "I am cold" under the very conditions under which Jones says it.

In this chapter I have been concerned with a single strand of Coval's argument. There are many others. For example, in addition to attempting to prove that the asymmetry of the first personal pronoun is contingent, and hence does not constitute valid grounds for skepticism, Coval attacks skepticism directly. His argument seems to me very powerful. If it collides with my contention that a person's conception of himself as a totality is asymmetrical, my only comment is that the collision is interesting in its own right. Like the feat of standing outside oneself to point to oneself, and like that of speaking of oneself, this collision evinces the self as a presupposition of the use of the first personal pronoun.

5 · ON THE TALL NAPOLEON

A part of a person is a manifest absurdity—Reid

Among the concepts with which the self has traditionally been associated are those of freedom, responsibility, and guilt. It is natural to formulate such concepts in terms of counterfactual conditionals. One version of freedom, for example, is "If I had chosen to do *X,* I could have done *X.*" One version of guilt is "If I had not done *X,* it would have been better." In this chapter I want to examine these counterfactuals and others which, like them, express what persons might have done instead of what they did do, or what they might have been instead of what they are. One purpose in doing so is to shed light on the relation that actually obtains between the self and freedom, responsibility, and guilt.

Some counterfactuals presuppose statements of the form "There could be an *A* the same as *B* except . . ." An example is "If this match had been scratched, it would have lighted," which presupposes "There could be a match the same as this except scratched." We often use expressions of the form "*A* is the same as *B* except . . . ," and we fill in the dots by naming two or three respects in which *A* and *B* differ. "*A* is the same as *B* except . . ." should be contrasted with "*A* is similar to *B.*" When we use the latter expression, we need only be prepared to name one respect or a few in which *A* and *B* are similar; thus "The Nymphenberg Palace is similar to an igloo in that both provide shelter." But unless we were joking, we should never say "The Nymphenberg Palace is the same as an igloo except . . . ," because we would then have to name an indefinitely large number of respects in order to fill in the dots. The Nymphenberg Palace is the same as an igloo except that one is in Germany and the other in Alaska; one is large and the other small; one is made of stone and the other of ice; one is the erstwhile habitation of royalty and the other is the present habitation of nomads; and so on; and so on; and so on. This is indeed just a joke. It is also a contradiction, for the indefinitely long string of exceptions denies the force of "is the same as." The Nymphenberg Palace and an igloo are not the same at all, although they are in a certain specialized respect similar.

Someone might challenge my first example. He might say that "This match is the same as that except scratched" is just a joke. For the scratched match, having lighted, is in fact different from the unscratched one in an indefinitely large number of respects. This is true but irrelevant. For in order to compare the two matches with precision, it is sufficient to say, "They are the same except that one has been scratched." The "except" clause does in effect list an indefinitely large set of differences between the matches, but it lists *all* of these differences; there are no further exceptions. There is no similar way of summarizing the differences between the Nymphenberg Palace and an igloo.

We can say of two different matches that they are the same except that one has been scratched, and we can say that two houses are the same except for location. We say that two books are the same except that one has a red cover and a text that has been brought up to date. But to say that two persons are the same except . . . is very unnatural. No one objects to finding *similarities* between Lincoln and Kennedy, but one would not ordinarily be inclined to say, "Lincoln and Kennedy are the *same* except . . . ." Normally, *A* can be the same person as *B* only if *"A"* and *"B"* are different names of one person; and when they are, it does not make sense to say *"A* is the same as *B* except . . . ." To say of *different* persons that they are the same except . . . is to fall into a contradiction.

One way to justify our aversion to saying that two persons are the same except . . . is in terms of considerations implicit in the unity of the person. In the preceding chapters I have had occasion to point out this unity—a super-unity so cohesive that it is capable of absorbing a contradiction. Such super-unity is involved in the contradiction of knowing the right and doing the wrong; it is implicit in self-evasion; and it is the ground of the possibility of the contradiction of a person's ability to refer to himself by pointing to himself as a totality.

One way to account for the existence of these contradictions is to agree with Thomas Reid's statement quoted at the beginning of this chapter: a part of a person is a manifest absurdity. The contradiction of knowing the right and doing the wrong arises because we cannot within the person distinguish a part that knew what it was to do from a part that reports failure to do what it knew it was to do, although we can and indeed must make this distinction in the computer. The contradiction of self-evasion arises because we cannot distinguish a part of the person that takes a certain position from another part that flees from that position. The contradiction of self-reference arises from the impossibility of distinguishing between the person pointing at himself and what he points at. All contradictions generating the self have their source in the fact that the person is a monadic source of action.

If persons have no parts, their differences from one another cannot be described by comparing their parts. It follows that it would be very unnatural to declare one person the same as another except in certain parts. When things do have parts, on the other hand, this sort of declaration is natural: "This book is the same as that except that it has a red cover and the text has been brought up to date."

Not all declarations of the form "A is the same as B except . . ." are concerned with parts. Thus in "These slacks are the same as those except for being made of wool rather than cotton," it is material that is being compared rather than parts. It is obvious, however, that what is without parts could not be made of material, for material is divisible.[1] (Whether it has ultimately indivisible atoms we need not consider; no one would identify a person with such an atom.) In the case of "This match is the same as that except scratched," it is neither parts nor material which we are comparing, but exposure to a causative agent (scratching). However, what is not made of a material cannot be involved in a causal relationship; "X causes Y" presupposes a material of which X or Y is a modification. Consider "Heating causes expansion (of a material)"; "Fatigue (in the human body) causes accidents." Precisely when we are able to formulate such relationships without reference to materials, we have passed from causal to purely functional statements, as when we identify heating as an increase of molecular velocities, and see that expansion comes to the same thing. Here there is no longer a need to refer to the expanding material.

1. For supplementary suggestions as to why the person is not made out of any material, see J. Shaffer, "Persons and Their Bodies," *Philosophy Review*, Vol. LXXV, 1966, pp. 59–77.

Finally, it is worth considering whether a comparison of things with respect to their *properties* could result in the statement "X is the same as Y except for possessing property P_1 instead of property P_0." Perhaps it could. But in the case of persons it could not. Because persons are not made of material, they cannot be distinguished by virtue of their material. Hence they can be distinguished only by their properties. Of course persons can have properties in common, but each person has at least one distinctive property that overrides any inclination to regard him as being the same as others. This is the previously-discussed property of conceiving himself as a totality in a distinctive way. It is this property alone that guarantees the spatiotemporal integrity of the person. Of two houses we can say "This is the same as that, except that it has been built at a different location." But we would never say that of two persons "Smith and Brown are the same except that Smith is here and Brown is there," because being here would not make Brown Smith. Brown is Brown wherever he is by virtue of a property that he shares with no one else.

It may be objected that the distinctiveness of Smith and Brown rests simply on their individuality rather than on the conception that each has of himself. There is a metaphysics of individuals according to which all individuals are distinct, whether they be persons, houses, books, stars, or atoms. The question, though, is "Under what circumstances do we invoke this metaphysics?" We invoke it in situations in which it is unnatural to consider things the same. To say that persons are individuals is just to say that we cannot regard them as the same. On occasion, we are inclined also to regard houses, matches, and books as individuals and as thus subject to the metaphysics of individuals. If I have been invited to Wilson's house, it is of no use to me to find a house that is the same but at a different location. If I seek the one unlighted match I have in my trousers pocket, it avails me little to find one that is the same but scratched. In each case, however, the invocation of the metaphysics of individuals is occasioned by a prior need to distinguish the individuals concerned. In the case of persons, the need arises from the fact that individuals identify *themselves*. Each has his own conception of himself, which is different from anyone else's self-conception. In Chapter 6 I will develop this thesis in detail, and my argument there will be an attempt to establish, by means of considerations somewhat different from the ones I have appealed to here, that the person is a monadic unity without parts.

Under some circumstances, we do say that different persons are the same; but when we do we are not thinking of them as persons, but rather as things either with parts or made of material or subject to causal interactions. Imagine a conference that is taking place on the fifteenth story of a building. None of the participants is the same as any other. But if two of them should jump out of a window they would become the same; the most talented participant and the least talented are the same, except in respects that are without importance, when both are falling toward certain death. What has happened here is that all the differences between the two have paled into insignificance before the fact of their sameness as falling bodies. This sameness can reach back through the window to embrace those still in the room. For Smith, who did not jump, is in fact the same as Brown, except that Brown did jump; there, but for the grace of God, goes Smith. Gravity is one of the great equalizers, in the sense that when persons are doomed by it, their differences become negligible.

Sometimes we are speaking somewhat with tongue in cheek when we talk of the sameness of persons. The woman who says "Men are all the same" is probably exaggerating, but she is not speaking figuratively; what she means is that most men, if not all, literally want the same thing, and their differences pale into insignificance before this identity in motivation. To say this is to regard men as less than persons, just as to emphasize the sameness of falling individuals is to regard them as less than persons.

I turn now to some counterfactual conditionals. Consider "If this match had been scratched, it would have lighted." This conditional clearly presupposes that there could be a match the same as this except scratched; if there could not be, the requisite lawlike connection between antecedent and consequent[2] would surely be lacking. Note that the conditional presupposes much more than merely that there could be a match *similar* to this. For a match could perfectly well be similar to this (say, in length) and yet not light when scratched (because it might have a head of the wrong composition).

---

2. See Nelson Goodman, *Fact, Fiction & Forecast,* Cambridge, Harvard University Press, 1955, p. 27.

The counterfactual "If Smith had jumped out of the window, he would have been killed" can be analyzed in a similar fashion. It presupposes that there could be a person the same as Smith, except having jumped. The Brown mentioned a few paragraphs back is such a person. Brown is not merely *similar* to Smith. All persons are *the same* in free fall.

But consider "If Napoleon had been six feet tall, he would (would not) have been just as great a soldier." On the analogy of the two previous examples, this presupposes that there could be a person the same as Napoleon except six feet tall. However, to say of Napoleon and someone six feet tall that they are the same is to fall into a contradiction; for in the absence of equalizers, no one but Napoleon can be the same as Napoleon. Since "There could be a person the same as Napoleon except six feet tall" is a contradiction, the counterfactual conditional that presupposes it is itself a contradiction.

Of course, what is self-contradictory is the proposition that there could be *another* person the same as Napoleon except six feet tall. A crucial objection consists in asking whether this must necessarily be the case. Is it not sufficient to hold that "If Napoleon had been six feet tall . . ." presupposes that there could have been a person *numerically identical* with Napoleon but six feet tall? But this is hardly a presupposition; it is just a paraphrase of the antecedent of the conditional. If there could have been a person numerically identical with Napoleon but six feet tall, he would (would not) have been just as great a soldier. In order to see why the conditional in question presupposes what it does, consider again the case of "If this match had been scratched, it would have lighted." I have already referred to the lawlike connection that must exist between the antecedent and consequent of this conditional. In the absence of this connection, there is no ground whatever for either asserting or denying the conditional. But clearly no such connection could be confirmed if there were no *other* match the same as this one in the relevant way. Hence if we are to make sense of the conditional at all we must assume that there could be *another* match the same as this except scratched. Similarly, if we are to make any sense at all of the conditional about Napoleon, we must assume that there could be *another* person the same as he except six feet tall. *This* presupposition, as I have shown, is self-contradictory; but at least it is meaningful, as the conditional itself could not be if it were not taken to imply the presupposition. In other words, the conditional can be meaningful only on the condition that it implies a contradiction, and so is itself a contradiction.

Not all counterfactual conditionals having "If Smith had jumped out of the window" as the antecedent are consistent. Thus "If Smith had jumped out of the window, he would have regretted it on the way down" does not appeal to gravity, or anything else, as an equalizer. It presupposes that there could be someone the same as Smith except having jumped, but refers to no crisis in which all others would be the same as Smith. Hence it—like "If Napoleon had been six feet tall he would (would not) have been just as great a soldier"—is inconsistent. Notice that it is the consequent that conveys the notion of an equalizer, such as sudden death; for the consistent conditional and the inconsistent one differ only in consequent. By changing the consequent, we can in fact formulate a *consistent* counterfactual about Napoleon: to wit, "If Napoleon had been six feet tall, he would have been 72 inches tall." Analytic truth is thus an equalizer. It is only in the absence of all equalizers that a counterfactual about a person is inconsistent.

It might seem that in asserting that in the absence of equalizers sameness does not apply to persons, I have espoused the nonsensical position of denying that a person can change. Jones was poor, but now he is rich. Is he not, then, "the same as Jones, except rich"? There would be a contradiction if "Jones" could only be interpreted as naming the past Jones; for no one could be the same as the past Jones except rich. But in fact "Jones" is the name of the person who both was poor in the past and is rich in the present. That person is the same as the then poor Jones *and* the same as the now rich Jones. Hence, although it is true that "the same as Jones except rich" is self-contradictory when "Jones" is interpreted as simply the past Jones, the contradiction can be removed by saying instead "the same as Jones past and present, except rich." Now, of course, the "except" is once again out of place—this time because "except rich" is redundant rather than because it is inconsistent. Rich or poor, Jones is Jones, but we cannot say "Tall or short, Napoleon is Napoleon," because there simply never was a tall Napoleon; there could thus be no one the same as Napoleon except tall.

What if future scholarship should establish that Napoleon was in fact six feet tall? The conditional "If Napoleon had been six feet tall . . ." would still be self-contradictory. For in addition to presupposing "There could be someone the same as Napoleon except six feet tall," it also presupposes "Napoleon was *not* six feet tall." This latter presupposition would, however, contradict what by hypothesis future scholarship is to have established.

I want now to apply this analysis to the concept of responsibility. It might be argued that my entire position rests on this concept but does it scant justice. The argument would run as follows: I have spoken of the self as the acceptance of a burden. One could agree with this characterization, but yet feel that I have characterized the burden in terms that are far too restrictive. Must the burden be a *contradiction*? It is not often that one must accept a contradiction, if indeed it is ever the case. Why not simply say that the burden that evokes the self is a *responsibility*? Notice that the same reciprocity claimed by me to hold between the self and a contradiction would also hold between the self and a responsibility. Just as I have argued that the self is evoked by precisely the contradiction it acknowledges, so it might be argued that the self is evoked by precisely the responsibility it acknowledges. Just as there is no pragmatic contradiction except in an individual's conjoint assertion of two mutually inconsistent propositions, there is no responsibility except for the individual willing to assume it. A responsibility acknowledged by no one is not a responsibility at all. At best, it is just a chore—a task defined by the rules alone, just as a merely syntactical contradiction acquires its status entirely from rules.

In reply, let me first say that I agree that the self is related to responsibility exactly as it is to contradiction. Yet contradiction is the more fundamental concept, for the acceptance of any responsibility rests upon the acceptance of a contradiction. Consider the statement "I am responsible for that misunderstanding." This presupposes "If I had acted or spoken differently, that misunderstanding would not have occurred." This in turn, as we have seen, presupposes "There could be someone the same as me except having acted or spoken differently on a certain occasion." This is a contradiction. I must accept *it* if I am to accept the statement about my responsibility. If I do not accept it, I shall be in the position of supposing that I could *not* have acted or spoken differently, so that the misunderstanding was unavoidable. But if it was unavoidable, I am not responsible.

The statement I have just analyzed refers to my responsibility for a past episode. It establishes that responsibility in retrospect. But this is the only way in which responsibilities can be established at all. It is only after the event for which I was responsible that I *see* that I was responsible, because it is only after the event that I can frame the requisite contrary-to-fact conditional. *Before* the event, the conditional would not be contrary to fact, and there is no contradiction. The idea of "Someone the same as me except having done X" is inconsistent only if X has not been done, and it is too late to do it. If it is not too late, perhaps I *will* do it, in which case "except having done X" will be redundant rather than inconsistent.

It may seem that I am arguing in a circle. I am trying to prove that all responsibilities are at root contradictions. This seems to be true of responsibilities retrospectively acknowledged. But when I consider the possibility of a nonretrospective responsibility, I appear to be saying "This is not a responsibility *because it is not inconsistent.*" But in fact there is independent evidence for holding that it is only after the event for which I was responsible that I see that I was responsible. Suppose I say to myself "I am responsible to see that there is no misunderstanding." I can accept this responsibility only because I can in imagination enact the consequences of not accepting it. I can imagine a situation in which I will be saying to myself "If I had acted or spoken differently, that misunderstanding would not have occurred." If I were incapable of imagining such a situation, it would simply not make sense to talk about my assuming responsibility. Primarily, then, responsibility is established retrospectively, and when it is established with respect to some present or future event, this depends upon our supposing that if we do not act in certain ways (or if we do) certain retrospective judgments will then be thrust upon us. In many cases we do not and can not foresee the consequences of our action or inaction. In such cases it is not possible for us to accept responsibility except in retrospect. It is only by regarding retrospective responsibility as primitive that we can adequately accommodate these cases as well as the others.

Responsibility presupposes the unity of the person because it requires the envisagement of one and the same person not having done X and yet having been able to do X. If it were merely the case that one person, Smith, had not done X but that another person, Jones, had been able to do X, we would not say that Smith's responsibility was to do X. It is only because we can identify Smith and Jones that we can hold Smith responsible. This identification is implicit in traditional theories of the person. Locke, for example, thought of the person as the locus of appropriate reward and punishment, and hence of responsibility. There are occasions, Locke saw, when we cannot identify the perpetrator of an act with a person who might not have performed the act, as when the perpetrator is insane. In such cases, "the same man would at different times make different persons."[3] In other words, the person for Locke has an absolute identity in terms of which alone it is appropriate to reward or punish him. If the person could change, he could shed his responsibilities, and it would then be unjust to punish him. But clearly punishment is sometimes just. Only the man changes; the person remains identical throughout his life unless some crisis in his mental health forces us to suppose that one person has replaced another in the same man.

What Locke and his successors did not see is that to regard the person as the locus of responsibility is to regard him not merely as a monad but as an inconsistent monad. To the sane perpetrator of an act it is not possible to attribute the schizophrenia that we attribute to the mad perpetrator when we say that he is two persons in one man. If we are to make sense of the proposition that A is responsible for having done X then we are required to suppose that there could have been someone *the same as A* but not having done X. Only by meeting this requirement can we judge whether the counterfactual that formulates A's responsibility—specifically, "If A had not done X, such and such would have happened"—is true or false. But the requirement, as we have seen, is inconsistent. There could *not* be anyone the same as A but not having done X.

When an act is insane, then, as Locke says, we distinguish its perpetrator from another person in the sane man who might have refrained from it. When it is sane, we do not make this distinction. Hence the ultimate criterion of whether there is one person or two is the sanity of the act. This presupposes that there is some reliable way of distinguishing sane from insane acts apart from what we know of the perpetrator. This is a difficult doctrine to maintain; especially since the difference may be one of degree only. The view that I am putting forward does not seem to me to involve these

3. *An Essay Concerning Human Understanding,* Book II, Chapter XXVII, Section 20.

difficulties. It is that whatever act we choose, whether sane or insane, we can distinguish its perpetrator from another person in the same man who might have refrained from it. Then, on the basis of what we know about the perpetrator, we can decide whether to identify him with the might-have-been nonperpetrator. The identification is always inconsistent, but such is the price we must pay for holding the perpetrator responsible. A person is not responsible merely because he has done something; he is responsible only if he can maintain an ecstatic unity with someone who might have acted otherwise. (Of course, I am using "ecstatic" here in a technical sense; ecstatic unity is marked by tension, not ecstasy. It is the mark of the insane man that he cannot maintain this unity.) Sanity involves a tension which in insanity goes slack or becomes a mechanical caricature of itself.

The counterfactual is a vehicle of reflection. It is needed to formulate the world of might-have-been in which the person must locate himself in order to form an idea of what he actually is. One important dimension of this world is guilt, the impression that one has failed to carry out a responsibility or some set of responsibilities. The formula of guilt, as I have already indicated, is "If I had not done X, it would have been better." This implies that there could have been a person the same as me except not having done X; and in my guilty reflections I constantly envisage that person and constantly make the futile attempt to acquire his identity. In pathological cases, and in the dreams of even non-pathological dreamers, this constant envisagement can take the form of *repetition,* the mechanism of which was first explained by Freud.[4]

Deliberation, as Aristotle saw, concerns the future.[5] It can be formulated in conditionals that are not counterfactual: "If I do X, it will be better." Guilt is deliberation inconsistently brought to bear on the past. Even the trivial guilt of the keypunch operator mentioned in Chapter 1—a guilt expressed by saying "Confound it! I knew I should have put that parenthesis in!"—is in effect a deliberation about the past. This exclamation contrasts with "I know I should put that parenthesis in" which expresses a straight-forward if trivial deliberation concerning the future. The force of the use of the past tense of "know" is to introduce into the past

4. Sigmund Freud, *Beyond the Pleasure Principle,* tr. Strachey, London, The Hogarth Press, 1950, Ch. IV.
5. This is clearly implied by *Nicomachean Ethics,* III, 3.

an efficacy intended to transform it magically into what might have been.

A book about the self should contain at least a short paragraph about freedom. My argument is that the self is not an organ of freedom—not an agency through which I am enabled to evade physical laws—but rather arises on the occasion of reflections about freedom, unifying the poles of the contradiction expressed by saying "There could have been a person the same as I except having chosen otherwise, but no other person is the same as I." Such reflections, however, rarely if ever enter into our daily lives. Although responsibility and guilt are integral to the fabric of everyday experience, freedom remains a speculative idea. It is of minor importance as an evoker of the self.

Yet freedom does have importance at another level. As a reflective grasp of the moral dimension of my existence, it is implicit in all my action. To act is always to raise the question of having acted otherwise. As Sartre once contended, man is condemned to be free. To be a man is to be the unity of what is and what might have been.

In this chapter I have written of actual and possible persons. The counterfactuals that formulate responsibility, guilt, and freedom presuppose the inconsistent identification of an actual person with a possible person who is the same. In explaining why I thought this identification was inconsistent I have been arguing, in effect, that the person is fully actual. He contains no possibilities, and there are no merely possible persons. I will say more concerning the first of these points before going on to discuss the second.

That a person contains no possibilities is simply a way of formulating his monadological character. How is this possibility-free character reflected in our common attitudes toward persons? Can a being without possibilities qualify as a person at all? It might seem that such a being could at most be a parody of a person—a zombie. But even if persons do not *contain* possibilities, they can still be related to them. The possibilities to which a person is related are outside as a horizon toward which he constantly tends. They are a constant threat to his full actuality. A person's possibilities hang over him like a thundercloud, and the cloud is the self.

From a more technical standpoint, we can formulate the relation between a person and his possibilities as a case of self-evasion.

A person both occupies a certain position—his full actuality—and withdraws from that position toward his possibilities. At any moment in his life, a person is complete. We do not usually regard a child as an incomplete adult; we meet him on his own terms, taking him for what he is. Yet the very completeness of the person is sustained by the threat of an advance on his part which could reveal the present stage of his development as merely a stage of his development. A person whose full actuality is not threatened by further possibilities collapses into a nonperson. His self evaporates.

In denying that the person has possibilities, there is one misunderstanding I wish to avoid. Even as fully actual, the person exhibits dispositions. He is irascible or kind. And dispositions are clearly sets of possibilities. "If you had called Smith by his first name, he would have been very angry"—this counterfactual asserts anger as a possibility of Smith. Notice, though, that dispositions depend on psychological mechanisms, and that such mechanisms are equalizers. What Smith will do if he has a certain disposition is, in effect, exactly what Jones will do if he has the same disposition; Smith and Jones are the same. But to treat them as the same is to treat them as less than persons. Furthermore, the possibilities that haunt a person are possibilities of *changing* in disposition rather than possibilities defined *by* a disposition. If his irascibility depersonalizes Smith, what restores his status as a person is the possibility of overcoming his irascibility—or the possibility that his irascibility will develop into an unmanageable fury. But the preemptive character of Smith's present irascibility prevents our envisaging either the self-control or the fury as possibilities, except in a horizonal way.

I turn from the discussion of whether persons have possibilities to the discussion of whether there are possible persons. The second question arises from a consideration of counterfactuals that make a claim even more radical than the claim made by saying, for example, "If I had acted differently, that misunderstanding would not have occurred." Examples can be generated by formulating "I'm sorry I was ever born" and "I'm glad I was born" as counterfactuals: "If I had not been born, it would have been (better) (worse) for me." A third-person example is Christ's comment, "Woe unto that man by whom the Son of man is betrayed! It had been good for that man if he had not been born!"[6]

6. Matthew 26:24.

I want to argue that counterfactuals like these are both inconsistent and necessary, and thus evoke the self. One way to begin is to
point out that persons and accidents have much in common. As Ryle
points out, if a highway engineer claims that a road improvement
he has designed has sharply reduced the number of accidents on the
road, you cannot ask him to substantiate this claim by listing the
accidents he has prevented.[7] Similarly, we cannot list the persons
who have not come into existence as the result of improved birth-
control techniques. We cannot name even one of them. Of course, we
can supply names that might have been used if more people had been
born than were actually born; but these are not the names of nonexis-
tent persons. A person cannot be named at all until he exists, at
least in the sense of having been conceived.

The following counterexample might be offered. Suppose that
a couple has a son every eighteen months, and that they have
decided to name their sons "Allen," "Bernard," "Clark," "David,"
and so on, in that order. Now assume that for some reason the sixth
son is not conceived. Can we say that something has happened
to prevent Frederick from coming into existence? If this means that
something has happened to prevent the *use* of the name "Frederick," this statement is acceptable although somewhat coy. But
if it means what it literally says—that Frederick, who never existed,
has been prevented from existing—it is sheer nonsense. We cannot
refer to Frederick at all until he has at least been conceived.[8]

I do not wish to deny that we *ever* refer to a person before he
is conceived. At the horizon of the daily life of many people is
a set of persons, some regarded as mythical and some as real, who
were referred to before they were conceived, in such scenes as the
Annunciation and Merlin's act of reserving the Siege Perilous at
King Arthur's Round Table for an as yet unknown occupant. The
idea of such a prefigured person has always been fascinating. What
one finds fascinating is the contrast between the person who is
prefigured, and hence is possible before being conceived, and the
vast majority of men who before they are conceived cannot be
envisaged as possibilities. It is important to remember that in
all historical ages, the ordinary person has regarded himself as
accidental. The evidence for this is precisely the way in which he

---

7. *Dilemmas*, Cambridge, Cambridge University Press, 1954, pp. 24–25.
8. In *The Language of Time* (New York, Humanities Press, 1968), Richard Gale
uses some similar examples, and concludes that "we cannot *successfully* use a
singular identifying expression—a proper name, definite description, or demon-
strative—to identify a future individual" (p. 183).

has been fascinated by the idea of a prefigured person—not only by Galahad and Jesus, but also by Oedipus and Isaac. The reason why this is important to remember is that we might be tempted to suppose that the idea that the average person is accidental arises from relatively recent discoveries in genetics—the discovery, for instance, that which of a staggering number of spermatozoa will fertilize the ovum and thus determine the heredity of the embryo is a matter of chance. But no discovery of this kind is in fact required as the source of the view that the person is accidental. For even if heredity were not a matter of chance, the person would still be accidental. In *Brave New World*, Huxley describes procedures for eliminating chance from heredity. The result is that every person brought into existence is either an Alpha, a Beta, a Gamma, or a Delta. But Alphas, Betas, Gammas, and Deltas are *kinds* of persons. And even though, in Huxley's world, it can be predicted what *kind* of a person will result from a given biochemical procedure, it cannot be predicted what *person* will result. All that is meant by a person's heredity is a general set of conditions necessary perhaps for all of his deeds but sufficient for none of them. And yet it is a person's deeds, to the extent that they are relevant to his conception of himself as a totality, that set him apart from the others. To return to a previous example, Galahad's heredity can make him strong of arm and resolute of spirit, but it cannot in itself cause him to be the person who performs some specific act. And in fact Galahad is not identified by his heredity, but rather as the person who drew Balin's sword from the stone. Notice that although it may be possible to arrange for a person's heredity in advance, it is a task of a different order of magnitude to arrange for his deeds in advance. We can follow Huxley's quasi-biological explanations of how it is arranged what heredity a person is to have, but is there any followable account of how it could be arranged what deeds a person is to perform? In fact, no such account is ever attempted, for the prefigured person is always regarded as being under the sponsorship of a divine agency, which makes the arrangements in ways inscrutable to human beings. When it is denied that there are divine agencies concerned to arrange the deeds of ordinary persons, the implication is that ordinary persons are accidental; and it is for this reason, rather than for any reason connected with modern genetics, that the belief that all persons or most of them are accidental has been almost universally accepted.

But of course the prefigured person is accidental too, in his own way. Even though he can be referred to before he is *conceived,* he cannot be referred to before he *exists.* No one can say how far back in the womb of time the existence of Galahad was called for, but before that time there was not a possible Galahad waiting to be actualized. The difference between the ordinary and the pre-figured person is primarily a difference in the kind of accident responsible for bringing each into existence. One is created by a genetic accident, the other by a theological accident.

Whenever we can properly refer to a person, then, he exists or has existed. There are no merely possible persons. Every person is or was actual. Someone might object at this point, "We have a use for expressions like 'Jones is an actual person.' From this it follows that 'Jones is a possible person' must also be meaningful." But consider the circumstances under which we would say "Jones is an actual person." There is an occasion for this remark only if it has been supposed that Jones is a *fictitious* person. The remark apprises us that Jones exists in real life as well as in fiction. But "actual" in this context does not contrast with "possible." A ficti-tious person is not one who is merely possible. One could not set out to actualize a fictitious person as one might set out to actualize a set of blueprints. Using "actual" to mean "not merely possible," we can say that the fictitious person is every bit as actual as the real-life person. He fails to be actual only if "actual" means "real-life." An objector might say "This may be true of Hamlet and Alyosha Karamazov. Actuality can be conceded them. But what of countless cardboard figures in inferior fiction—the stereotyped heroes and villains? Are not *these* merely possible persons?" But if stereo-types are possible persons, it ought to be possible to conceive of their actualization. No doubt there are real-life persons who behave like stereotyped salesmen, lovers, and petty bureaucrats. But such behavior is never the actualization of an abstract pattern. It is not the personalization of stereotype. Rather, it is the result of the depersonalization of the person. What was once a concrete person has become abstract. Instead of supposing that a possibility has been actualized, we should see that an actuality has been possibilized. In this process of depersonalization, the man may in the end coincide with a fictitious stereotype. This result is funny or pathetic; but there is no reason why the actualization of a possibility should in itself be funny or pathetic.

The stereotype is not a possible person because the result of fleshing it out is never a person but precisely an impersonal being. The smiling housewife in the bowl cleaner ad could never be actual, because the actual person is not the actualization of any antecedent possibility. But various possibilities may be subsequent upon the person's actuality. We exhibit such possibilities when we make a caricature of an actual person. A caricature is not a blueprint; it pre-supposes the flesh-and-blood person. And a stereotype is a degenerate caricature. It is from the behavior of actual salesmen, lovers, and petty bureaucrats that stereotypes arise.

My argument that there are no merely possible persons has been lengthy, but it took us through some territory that was of interest in its own right. I return now to the thesis that required the argument to be constructed, specifically: that a counterfactual like "If I had not been born, it would have been (better) (worse) for me" is both inconsistent and necessary. Because this conditional presupposes "I might not have been born," and thus refers to a merely possible me, its inconsistency may be taken to have been established. I turn there-fore to the question of the necessity of conditionals of this sort.

It is a platitude that although men and animals alike exist, only men know that they themselves exist. An animal no doubt knows that various objects exist; that is, it is aware of their presence or absence. But an animal cannot be aware of its own existence. Not that it is insensate—the dog is surely familiar with its own odor and tactile qualities and the look of most of its own body. The difficulty is instead logical. In order to be aware of one's own existence, one would have to be capable of envisaging a contrasting state. But to envisage one's own nonexistence is precisely to think of oneself as an unactualized possibility.

Because all the animals except man are rational, limited to making consistent choices on the basis of what they perceive and of learned or innate patterns of response, they are unable to become aware of their own existence. In this respect they are like computers, which make consistent choices on the basis of input and program. A computer can no doubt be aware of its own states.[9] But it cannot formulate the idea of its own nonexistence, and hence, Richter's *New Yorker* cartoon[10] to the contrary notwithstanding, it can per-form no *cogito*. For similar reasons, the computer cannot rejoice

9. See Hilary Putnam, "Minds and Machines," reprinted in Anderson, ed., *Minds and Machines,* New York, Prentice-Hall, 1964; especially pp. 81–85.
10. *Ibid.*, frontispiece.

or sorrow over the fact of its own existence. That man is able to do this evinces one last human resource that has not been and cannot be duplicated in the computer—the capacity to come to terms with inconsistency.

Not only *can* a person know that he exists, but he *must* know it. I have said before that the very act by which a person refers to himself presupposes that he conceives of himself as a totality. This conception cannot be simply a person's image of his own feet, clothes, hands, and of the tip of his nose; for no such image serves to distinguish him from others. In order for his act of self-reference to be exclusive, it must implicate the person's awareness of his own existence, as conceived from a point of view from which such existence is merely possible. I spoke earlier of the strangeness of the situation in which a person points to himself. He seems to be outside himself. Precisely this ecstasis is required by every act of self-reference.

Every person, at least when he is not absorbed in a passive experience, must perform a non-Cartesian *cogito*. The point of this *cogito* is not that to doubt my existence I must exist as the doubter, but rather that the self arises in the very act of contemplating one's existence, since the act of contemplation can be carried out only from a vantage point beyond existence. The "ego" that Descartes discovered was in fact a thinking person, not a self. But the more radical *cogito* that we do in fact perform does yield a self.

Reflections expressed by means of counterfactuals beginning "If I had not been born . . ." can be classed together under the rubric of "The Problem of Birth." It is odd that although the corresponding Problem of Death has received considerable attention in the literature of philosophy, the Problem of Birth has received almost none. Yet it is precisely this problem that has begun the philosophical ruminations of many a child, wondering, for example, who he would have been if his parents had never met. It is not surprising that such ruminations should announce the appearance of the self.

6 · THE UNIQUENESS OF THE PERSON

What brings the self into philosophy is the fact that 'the world is my world.'—Wittgenstein

The analysis of counterfactuals concerning persons given in the last chapter—an analysis leading to the conclusion that in guilt, responsibility, and reflections on freedom the person assumes the burden of a contradiction—rests on a certain metaphysical view of the person. According to this view, persons are unique in a way in which things are not: of two persons *A* and *B* it cannot be asserted that "*A* is the same as *B* except. . . ." This metaphysical view was to some extent defended in Chapter 5. The defense rested, however, on a premise that needs much further clarification; the premise, to wit, that the uniqueness of the person depends on his view of himself as a totality. In the present chapter I will try to provide some systematic justification for this premise.

   The feeling that there is something unique about each person is articulated in many theological, philosophical, and legal systems. It has given rise, for example, both to the doctrine of the soul and to the concept of murder as the unpardonable act of destroying a unique individual. In philosophy, the contention that persons are not interchangeable has been formalized in terms of theories of personal identity which claim to show how in principle we could tell one person from another, and thus how to avoid supposing that they could be interchanged. The identity of the person has usually been taken to pose a problem distinct from that of the identity of a physical object or organism. It is supposed that persons are unique in a stronger sense than things. Thus Locke distinguishes the identity of the person from that of the man.[1] There is a question, however,

1. *An Essay Concerning Human Understanding*, Bk. II, Ch. 27, §§6ff.

whether traditional theories of personal identity do justice to this stronger uniqueness. Some of them begin by neglecting the very consideration that makes personal identity a distinctive problem; they define personal identity simply as the physical identity of the person. On this point, Sydney Shoemaker[2] writes:

> People sometimes become puzzled by the notion of personal identity on being told that during any seven year period (or so) all the molecules in a human body are replaced by different ones. Clearly, anyone who is puzzled by the notion of personal identity for this reason should be equally puzzled by the identity of dogs and oak trees.

Other theories define personal identity in terms of memory; let us consider in turn theories of these types.

According to the theory that equates personal with physical identity, the career of the person from birth to death is precisely the space-time career of his body during that period, or else can be exactly correlated with that career. Hence a person can always be identified by means of a singular description referring to the space-time career. Thus "the killer of Martin Luther King, Jr." refers to a person who at one stage of his body's career fired a shot from a flophouse in Memphis.[3] At a later date, if some person's body can be shown to be carrying out a career continuous with the career of the body in the flophouse, that person can then be identified as the killer of Martin Luther King, Jr.

A singular description can refer to a space-time career only if the properties in terms of which it is formulated are all *objective*. A property is "objective" in the broad sense in which I am using the term when, and only when, there is a way of finding out whether a person or thing has that property. Thus if I say "Jones is the man in the red coat" I have identified him in terms of an objective property. But if I say "Jones is the man thinking of Waukegan," I may not have succeeded in referring to a space-time career, because it may be impossible to find out who, if anyone, is thinking of Waukegan. The man may tell us what he is thinking of, but he may not.

It is obvious that on this theory personal identity is simply a case of identity in general. The man who killed Martin Luther King,

2. *Self-Knowledge and Self-Identity*, Ithaca, N. Y., Cornell University Press, 1963, pp. 5–6.
3. This was written at a time before the killer of Dr. King was identified, but it does not seem worthwhile to change the example.

Jr. and the bullet that killed Martin Luther King, Jr. differ mainly in the complexity of their careers. I want to consider now whether this theory is an acceptable solution to the problem which I am presuming it is intended to solve; namely, the problem of accounting for the uniqueness of the person.

In many cases, to be sure, a person's ascription of uniqueness to another or to himself is a claim entirely formulated in terms of objective properties—what I will call an objective claim. Consider "Smith holds the record for the 100-yard dash at Jones Junior High," "Wilberforce Snodgrass is the only person in the world of that name," "I am the only person who was born at Mercy Hospital on June 11, 1917," and "I am the only person in the world with these particular fingerprints." We know what would be involved in verifying or disconfirming any of these statements. Even "I am the only person now standing here" is objective, in spite of being analytically true (at least for certain interpretations of its terms), since there is a way (a very easy way) of ascertaining whether it is true or false.

Yet a person can ascribe uniqueness to another or to himself without making an objective claim at all. That this is the case is implied by the fact that one might regard the uniqueness claimed in each of the examples I have just given, or in any objective statement at all, as completely trivial in comparison with a more important way in which the person in question is unique. Clearly, Smith will continue to be the unique person he is even after his record for the 100-yard dash is broken, and the uniqueness of Snodgrass would not in the least be diminished by the discovery of a namesake. If someone else should turn up with exactly my fingerprints, I would worry about his leaving some of these prints at the scenes of crimes, but I certainly would not regard the duplication as a challenge to my own claim to uniqueness. The case of "I am the only person now standing here" is more difficult to dispose of, because it is impossible to conceive of its being false; but surely a person need not feel his uniqueness to be *defined* by his spatiotemporal exclusiveness. It is not the fact that I am the only person now standing here that makes me unique. If you were now standing where I am in fact now standing, you would still not be I.

If a claim to uniqueness is objective, it must specify the respect in which uniqueness is claimed; otherwise there is no way of finding out whether it is true or false. The moon is unique *as a natural satellite of the earth,* and Smith is unique *as a Jones Junior High sprinter.* If I am claiming that I am objectively unique, I must assert that I am unique *as the only person who was born at Mercy Hospital on June 11, 1917, as the sole possessor of these particular finger-prints,* or in some other particular respect or respects. If I cannot specify any respect in which I claim to be unique, or if I reject every putative specification, then there is no way of finding out whether my claim is true or false, and hence it is not objective. It seems clear, however, that a person claiming to be unique can reject every puta-tive specification of his claim to uniqueness. Thus whatever the facts about me—my name, age, build, place and date of birth, finger-prints, achievements, or police record—I can reject any statement to the effect that these facts, together or in any combination, consti-tute my uniqueness. Hence my claim to uniqueness need not be objective.

I conclude that the theory that equates personal with physical identity fails to do justice to the person's intimations of his own uniqueness. For that matter, as we shall see, there are claims of uniqueness put forward on behalf of another person to which this theory fails to do justice. I turn now to the theory that sees mem-ory as the foundation of personal identity. This theory can be expounded in terms of an example. If a woman claims to be Ana-stasia, daughter of the last Czar, she can strengthen her claim to the extent that she can remember incidents in which Anastasia was involved but which persons outside Anastasia's household would have no occasion to know about. This theory becomes operative when there are gaps in what is known of the space-time career of a person. But there almost always are such gaps; we cannot be constantly monitored by others.

It is difficult to be clear to what extent this is an autonomous theory. When we have succeeded in monitoring another person, the physical identity theory takes precedence; we do not accept his state-ment that he remembers being at *A* when we saw him at *B*. If we believe in reincarnation, however, we allow for exceptions to the precedence of the physical identity theory. Another respect in which the memory theory may not be autonomous is that we can sometimes find out what a person remembers by asking him, so that his memo-ries, or at least his recitals of them, can constitute objective proper-ties by which he is characterized. Also, what a person remembers can be partly the result of inference. I *think* I went to the post office before I went to the hardware store, but I see now that this could not have been the case, because they do not cash checks at the post office. When I remember in this way I am really editing my memory-images on the basis of what I know about the space-time career of my own body.

A person's memories can, however, be noninferential. This is a point made with telling force by Sydney Shoemaker.[4] I can *remember* having gone for a walk without *reaching the conclusion* that I went for a walk. When we emphasize noninferential memory, and play down the importance of a person's *telling* his memories as an objective performance, we approach a theory of personal identity which, unlike the physical identity theory, is not based upon objective properties. According to this new theory, the person is identified with the sum of his noninferential memories.

Whoever attempts to defend this theory is in grave danger of being thrust back into the physical identity theory, for he is sure to be confronted with the statement that memories can be illusory even if they are noninferential (my noninferential memory of having gone for a walk may in fact be mistaken). If he admits this possibility, and attempts to formulate a criterion for distinguishing illusory from veridical noninferential memories, he will find himself talking about objective properties. Hence if he wishes to make a definite move away from the physical theory, he must stop supposing that there is any important difference between illusory and veridical memories. He must hold that the two kinds are equally eligible to be components of the sum of noninferential memories that makes up the person. In this case, their significance as *memories* fades. It is not their reference to a real or fancied past that qualifies them as eligible, but simply the fact that they are among the contents of consciousness. This view, however, is in essence just Locke's doctrine that personal identity is a persistence of consciousness.[5] Against this analysis, I believe that the objections of Butler[6] and Reid[7] are valid. To begin with, we are continuously a person, but our consciousness is not continuous. Furthermore, Reid uses the example of the "brave officer" to argue that even if our consciousness were continuous from birth to death, it could fail to include episodes early in our life, and such episodes, according to Locke's doctrine, would then have to be

---

4. *Op. cit.,* especially Chapter 4.
5. *Essay,* Bk. II, Ch. XXVII, pp. 6–10.
6. *Dissertation I*—Of Personal Identity.
7. *Essays on the Intellectual Powers of Man,* Essay III, Chapter III.

assigned to a different person. Again, Locke confuses personal identity with the *evidence* we have of our personal identity. Even if, as Reid suggests, by "consciousness" Locke means "memory," my identity does not *consist* in what I remember. Reid also asks, "Is it not strange that the sameness or identity of a person should consist in a thing *which is continually changing,* and is not any two minutes the same?"[8]

The physical identity theory, then, does not provide an adequate account of the strong sense of uniqueness that is thought to apply to persons rather than things. The memory theory either collapses into the physical identity theory or else is incoherent in its own terms. Yet it is a step in the right direction. There is hope only for a view that refuses to identify the person in terms of objective properties. The real difficulty with the memory theory is that it conceives nonobjective properties too narrowly, limiting them to fugitive contents of consciousness. I want now to sketch out a view in which the uniqueness of the person is more adequately construed in nonobjective terms.

I begin by noting that "X is unique" can express a nonobjective claim whether X is a thing or a person. It is helpful to consider such a claim first as it applies to a thing. One of the ways in which a thing might be unique is in being irreplaceable. Of course a unique thing need not be irreplaceable—the one and only desk in my room could easily be replaced by another. On the other hand, anything irreplaceable would necessarily be unique, at least in the sense of being the only one obtainable. In any event, sometimes we regard a thing as unique in the sense of being irreplaceable. Now irreplaceability can be either objective or nonobjective. Sometimes when we regard a thing as irreplaceable, we are supposing its irreplaceability to have the status of a fact. There are ways of finding out whether the head gasket of a 1933 Packard is replaceable or not. But sometimes the irreplaceability of a thing is a matter more of attitude than of fact. I say that this table is irreplaceable, although in fact three dozen tables exactly like it are in existence. What I mean is that this table is an heirloom, and that if it were lost or destroyed none of the other three dozen could take its place in my personal scheme of things. Of course it is a fact that it is an heirloom. But my decision to honor its status as an heirloom by refusing to accept any substitute is not entailed by the fact that it is an heirloom. I *can*

8. *Ibid.,* p. 251.

forget all about its status, and think of it as just a common table. On the other hand, I could have treated the table as an heirloom even if it had not really been one; I might have made a mistake about its origin. That my assertion of irreplaceability expresses an attitude on my part rather than an objective claim is shown by the consideration that if I am mistaken about the origin of the table, it is not inconsistent of me to continue declaring its irreplaceability, even after my mistake is pointed out to me. I may have come to take a fancy to this particular table. Of course it is more probable that once I see that the table in question is not the heirloom I thought it was, I will withdraw my ascription of irreplaceability to it. Such a withdrawal may be dictated by a sense of the appropriate; it is ridiculous to get involved with a thing with which one has, after all, no real connection. But the withdrawal is not dictated by the requirements of logical consistency; for it is not *inconsistent* of me to continue to consider the table irreplaceable. On the other hand, when the ascription of irreplaceability to a thing expresses an objective claim rather than an attitude, logical consistency is the criterion. If when I say "This table is irreplaceable" I mean "There exists no table the same as this, and none can be obtained," then I *must* withdraw my statement if I find out that another table the same as this *does* exist or that another *can be* obtained. In practice, the situation is complicated because part of the meaning of "*A* is the same as *B*" can be that we take the same attitude toward *A* as we do toward *B*, while at the same time the attitude we take depends upon our belief regarding the sameness of *A* and *B*. Thus objective and attitudinal factors can and do interact. Our attitudes spring from what we take to be facts; for example, that this table is an heirloom. At the same time, the facts *about* our attitudes regarding things are among the facts about those things. From such facts further attitudes may spring.

The remarks I have just made are corroborated by familiar features of the collector's instinct. The collector seeks the original and spurns the copy. Of course, the original may in fact be intrinsically superior to any possible copy. In that case, its irreplaceability is a matter of fact, and the collector's attitude is highly appropriate. But in our Xerox Age, it becomes more and more plausible to suppose that a copy might exactly duplicate the original. Hence the claim to irreplaceability can be nonfactual. But it is still to be treated with the greatest respect.

When we assert that a given postage stamp has no duplicates, and then proceed to reject the alleged duplicates brought to us, there is a point beyond which our techniques of examination will not permit us to go. A plausible forgery is always possible. Such a forgery could replace the specimen in question in every detail that we are capable of discriminating, yet its existence would constitute no evidence whatever against the thesis that the stamp is irreplaceable. The stamp is irreplaceable only because we refuse to accept replacements for it.

It may be objected that even if the facts regarding the stamp's physical properties—its design, color, ink, watermark, and so on—are insufficient to establish its irreplaceability, there is another set of facts that can be called on which in themselves are sufficient. These are the facts of the history of the stamp. This objection, however, merely postpones the problem; namely, why the stamp is regarded as irreplaceable once we have traced its history. Not all stamps the history of which we can trace are thought to be irreplaceable.

Persons as well as things can be irreplaceable, and their irreplaceability can be a matter of attitude as well as one of objective fact. It is clear that when I call someone unique but refuse to consider any fact as relevant to my claim, all that I can possibly mean is that no one can take his place. Of course "his place" must be understood through reference to my attitude rather than to facts; in saying that no one could take his place, I do not mean to suggest that no one could in fact do what he does. I mean rather that I refuse, or am unable, to accept any substitute for him.

Even though I am not usually making an objective claim when I say that my friend is irreplaceable, facts can enter into my judgment, because my ascription of irreplaceability can be based on a belief regarding my friend's qualities. It may be because I suppose that my friend is uniquely talented and vital that he occupies a unique place in my affections. If later I come to see him as pallid and humdrum, I may well withdraw my ascription of irreplaceability to him. But I need not. I can in perfect consistency continue to regard him as irreplaceable, just as I can continue to regard the table as irreplaceable even when I learn that it is not an heirloom. Similarly, the mother's certainty that the infant handed to her in the maternity ward is irreplaceable arises from her belief that it is in fact hers. But if she insists that the infant is irreplaceable—not as a fact but as a matter of her attitude—even after it has been proved to her that there was a mistake in identity and that the infant is not in fact hers, she is not being inconsistent, although it would be inconsistent of her to persist in identifying the child as her own.

Let us speak of an ascription which is not primarily an objective claim, but is rather an expression of an attitude, as an *imputation*. We *impute* irreplaceability to persons and things to which we ascribe it nonobjectively. Imputed irreplaceability is obviously relative to the imputer. Someone else can impute irreplaceability to something to which I do not impute it and vice versa. Thus when irreplaceability is understood to be imputed, the sentence "X is irreplaceable" is not complete. To complete it, we must add ". . . in A's world." I know fairly well to what and to whom you impute irreplaceability, even though I do not myself necessarily impute irreplaceability to those same things and persons; they are irreplaceable in your world, but not necessarily in mine. *That* they are irreplaceable in your world is, of course, an objective property by which you are characterized. If we think of nonimputed irreplaceability—for example, the fact that this table cannot be replaced or the fact that a certain person cannot be replaced in a certain role—as a first-order fact, a fact about imputed irreplaceability can be thought of as a second-order fact. It is thus a second-order fact about me that A is irreplaceable in my world.

An imputation is an expression of an attitude. It is important to understand what attitude it expresses. If I impute irreplaceability to a person or thing, then there is often no doubt a sense in which I am *fond* of the object of my imputation. But I can be fond of something without missing it when it is gone: out of sight, out of mind. Surely, however, to regard something as irreplaceable is to feel certain that I will miss it when it is no longer available. It may seem that I am analyzing the imputation as a kind of prediction: I *will* miss the person or thing. A prediction, however, is hardly to be classed as an attitude. In any case, imputation is more than a prediction. I can easily feel sure that I will miss it when it is gone, without imputing irreplaceability to it. I may simply be addicted to it. In that case my prediction that I will miss it is simply an expression of its objective irreplaceability. It is in this sense that Linus's blanket in the *Peanuts* cartoons is irreplaceable.

We cannot analyze a case of imputed irreplaceability as either simply a fondness or simply a prediction. Nor can we analyze it as a combination of both. If I am fond of something, and predict that

I will miss it when it is no longer available, my prediction has the effect of bestowing upon my fondness the status of a fact. Instead of being the manifestation of a gratuitous imputation, my fondness becomes a property the presence or absence of which can be objectively tested by withdrawing the object, to ascertain whether I do in fact miss it.

Yet if I impute irreplaceability to a person or thing, I am fond of him or it, and I will miss the object of my affection when it is gone. But it can be true that I *will* miss it even though I do not *predict* that I will miss it. In other words, my imputation is a *disposition* on my part to miss the object when it is no longer available. Such a disposition is clearly an attitude on my part, not a fact about the object—an attitude characterized as a refusal to accept any substitute for the object. Such a refusal is more than a fondness, because it implies that I would miss the object were it withdrawn; but it is less than a prediction, because it does not imply that I *say* or *claim* that I would miss it. Indeed, it seems clear that I can refuse to accept a substitute for something without making any such statement or claim. As an attitude, the refusal characterizes me *now*. In order to be sure that I am fond of something I do not have to wait until it is gone and see whether I in fact miss it.

I have spoken of the time when the person or thing to which we impute irreplaceability might be gone, or might be withdrawn or no longer available. It is not easy to spell out these locutions precisely. Clearly, if we impute irreplaceability to something or someone, then it or he will be missed if totally and irrevocably destroyed. But this is trivially true, because it begs the question. Whether an act of destruction is regarded as irrevocable depends upon what we regard as irreplaceable. It is only because I refuse to accept a substitute for the table I am fond of that I would regard its destruction as irrevocable. Otherwise, I could be quite contented with a copy of the ruined table. An acceptable copy is a revocation; a loss is irrevocable only when no copy is acceptable. The same principle applies to persons. What it means to say that a person has been irrevocably destroyed is simply that we refuse to accept any substitute for him; otherwise, there is always the strong possibility that another person could take his place. This consideration affects the discussion of the personal survival of death. What does it mean to contend that a person *cannot* survive it? Any proof of this contention would depend upon the assumption that the person is irreplaceable in the first place. The logical point I am trying to make is illustrated by the following statement by Landsberg.[9]

> In primitive societies the individual is not sufficiently differentiated from his clan to be able to individualize himself in any other way than by his position in the clan and his function in the social organism. If, on his death, another individual succeeds to this position, the latter also acquires the name and soul of the dead person.

If I impute irreplaceability to a person or thing, however, my attitude need not be simply a disposition to miss him or it if totally and irrevocably destroyed. I can miss a person if he departs permanently or even temporarily. I can miss him if he leaves me for a day, but, under other circumstances, not miss him if he is absent for a week. I do not miss the table if I put it in storage, but I do miss it if I sell it to my next-door neighbor, even if I see it every day. Ownership is related in complex ways to the imputation of irreplaceability to inanimate things. We treat animals in this respect partly like things and partly like persons. As for persons, there are naturally many occasions on which the claim that a person is irreplaceable is not an imputation at all. The man who mows my lawn is *in fact* irreplaceable; if he should leave my employ, I am sure I could not get anyone to take his place. But I do not necessarily *impute* irreplaceability to him. On the other hand, I can perfectly well suppose that a person to whom I impute irreplaceability is replaceable in every role that he plays.[10]

I have been dealing in a loose way with two concepts: that of the nonobjective ascription of uniqueness to a thing or person, and that of the imputation of irreplaceability to it or him. I wish to argue now that every case of the former is a case of the latter; what uniqueness must mean, when it is not objective, is imputed irreplaceability. For if I claim that a thing or person is unique, but refuse to specify *any* respect in which it or he is unique, and reject every attempt on someone else's part to specify such a respect, the only interpretation that can possibly be put on my testimony is that I simply refuse or am unable to accept any substitute for the thing or

9. Paul–Louis Landsberg, "The Experience of Death," in Maurice Natanson, *Essays in Phenomenology*, The Hague, Martinus Nijhoff, 1966, p. 196.
10. The interplay of considerations affecting a person's replaceability and irreplaceability is superbly handled by Kuang-Ming Wu in his article "Are Persons Replaceable?", *Philosophy and Phenomenological Research*, Vol. XXIX, 1968, pp. 245–56.

person, without there being any reason for this refusal or incapacity. In other words, my attitude toward the thing or person is that it or he is simply irreplaceable. But this is exactly what it means to say that I impute irreplaceability to it or him.

I can regard *myself* as irreplaceable. Such a supposition might take the form of an objective claim of the first or second order. Thus it may be a fact that when I am gone, I cannot be replaced as an eye-witness of a certain historical event; or it may be a fact that I am irreplaceable in someone else's world. To such forms of irreplaceability there correspond forms of replaceability. Thus I may be convinced that I can be replaced either in fact or in the estimation of others. The first of these convictions is exemplified in the soldier who is sure that if he falls, another will rise to take his place. The second represents a kind of self-effacement that can be sincere, ironic, or pathological.

This brings us to the topic of the *imputation* of irreplaceability to oneself. I have already pointed out that there are intimations of one's uniqueness that are not reducible to any objective claim. I have said that whatever the facts about me—my name, age, build, place and date of birth, fingerprints, achievements, or police record—I can reject any statement to the effect that these facts, together or in any combination, constitute my uniqueness. And we have seen how the nonobjective ascription of uniqueness to a person or thing is tantamount to the imputation to him or it of irreplaceability. It follows that persons sometimes do impute irreplaceability to themselves. They can do so even when they suppose it to be both a first-order and a second-order fact that they are replaceable.

But *can* I impute irreplaceability to myself? If I impute it to X, then if X is destroyed, I miss X. Hence if I impute irreplaceability to myself, then if I am destroyed, I miss myself. But I can never miss myself, since I cannot be absent from myself. And I can be destroyed. Hence the conditional "If I am destroyed, I miss myself" is false. Hence I cannot impute irreplaceability to myself.

But I cannot impute replaceability to myself, either. For the statement that X is replaceable in A's world presupposes that X might either belong or not belong to A's world; that is, that A's world would continue to exist even in the absence of X. But clearly A's world cannot continue to exist in the absence of A. My world is one constantly characterized by my presence. I can, of course, attempt to imagine myself as absent from it, but if it be true that no one can literally imagine a contradiction—for example, a round square —then I must always fail in this attempt.

The conclusion is inescapable that although I can impute irreplaceability or replaceability to others, I can make no imputation at all concerning myself. This conclusion, however, is as absurd as it is inescapable. I am a person. Why should I be unable to make, vis-à-vis myself, the same judgments that I can make vis-à-vis others? If I suppose that someone else has a place in my world, can I not suppose that I, too, have a place in it? Am I to have no place at all except in another's world? Can I put no value on myself? The problem here is isomorphic with that of self-reference. It would be absurd if I could refer to anyone else by pointing to him but could not refer to myself by pointing to myself.

That I am a person at all is a paradox. The interests of logical consistency would best be served if I were *not* a person, and hence did not have to bear to myself relations that are in fact irreflexive. The relation in question is that borne by a person A to a person B in whose world A is replaceable or irreplaceable. We have noted other relations that can give rise to the paradox of being a person. All these relations are ones normally borne by a person to others. The paradox arises only when the relations are turned inward so that a person bears them to himself.

If the imputation of irreplaceability to oneself is a paradox, the self is called into existence to bring into a single focus the contradictory poles of the paradox. This act of synthesis requires no explanation beyond that given in Chapter 2. It is the same act that occurs both as consequence and as ground of any necessary paradox.

In this book, my main thesis so far has been that the self is the acceptance of a contradiction. One of the most plausible criticisms of this thesis is the following: Different persons can accept the same contradiction. From this it would seem to follow that different persons can have the same self. But any such conclusion contradicts a basic principle concerning the self; namely, that selves cannot be shared.[11] Indeed, it can be argued that the self is or ought to be defined precisely as the locus of the unshareable, as the source of the privacy of the perspective that each of us has. But even if we do not suppose that there is anything intrinsically unshareable or private in

11. I do not mean to suggest here that it is necessary to be a solipsist—to take the view that selves are radically unshareable. Many thinkers hold that unless selves are in part shared, they cannot be unshared, or private.

a person's perspective, each person is essentially different from all others; and his self, we may say, is the locus of the differences; at least, of those differences that are essential. The criticism I am considering really makes two points. The first is that any theory of the self ought to exhibit the self as the locus of the uniqueness of persons; for this is what the self fundamentally is. My view, in these terms, offends by its lack of concern for this fundamental property of what it professes to be characterizing. But it offends in an even worse way as well—and this is the second point. For it seems in fact to *deny* that a person's self is a locus of uniqueness. If all persons have the same self, this self could hardly serve to differentiate them.

I do in fact deny that the self is a locus of uniqueness, but this is only because I believe that the self and uniqueness are related in another way. The self is *evoked* by intimations of uniqueness. The uniqueness that evokes it is a predicate that applies in the first instance to persons, not selves. Yet I would certainly not agree that the self that each of us acquires in imputing irreplaceability to himself is the same as the self that everyone else acquires. For my self and your self differ in arising from different contradictions. *A*'s imputation of irreplaceability to himself implies "*A* is irreplaceable in *A*'s world." But *B*'s imputation implies "*B* is irreplaceable in *B*'s world." The two contradictions are as different as *A* is different from *B*. But it is precisely in order to declare the difference between *A* and, among others, *B,* that *A* claims that he is irreplaceable. If he is irreplaceable, then neither *B* nor anyone else can replace him, and it is in this respect that there is an essential difference between *A* and *B*. Since *A* and *B* are, at least by their own reckoning, essentially different, it follows that "*A* is irreplaceable in *A*'s world" cannot have the same meaning as "*B* is irreplaceable in *B*'s world."[12]

At least one serious question, however, remains. *A* can clearly know that *B* is irreplaceable in *B*'s world. Because "*B* is irreplaceable in *B*'s world" is, however, the occasion for the emergence of *B*'s self, does *A* then possess *B*'s self? To answer this question, we must distinguish between *A*'s imputation of irreplaceability to himself and his

12. If *A*'s world is a purely private world, and if the same is true of *B's* world, then it might seem that *A* and *B* have fallen into "private contradictions"— unavailable as contradictions to others. Whether "private contradictions" are contradictions at all is a serious question. In fact, however, *A*'s world is not purely private, and neither is *B's. A* can have a world only because he can in some way contrast it with *the* world which lies outside it. This point is developed in Chapter 10, where, instead of speaking of worlds, I speak of philosophical positions.

knowledge that *B* imputes irreplaceability to *him*self. The former is an imputation, the latter a second-order fact. One can *impute* irreplaceability only to things and persons in one's *own* world. *A* can impute irreplaceability to *B* in *A*'s world, but not in *B*'s world. The most *A* can claim with respect to *B* is: "*B* imputes irreplaceability to *B*." Now *B*'s position is, as we have seen, self-contradictory. But surely *A* does not contradict himself in *reporting B*'s position. It must be possible to talk about contradictions without contradicting oneself. That is all that *A* is doing in reporting the second-order fact that *B* takes a self-contradictory position. *A* cannot possibly take that position himself; for in order to do so he would have to impute to *B* irreplaceability *in B*'s *world*. Of course *A*, if he is thoughtful, sees that *B* has a self. But he cannot *acquire B*'s self. The only self that he can acquire is his own.

I turn to a further objection. Granted that a case can be made for supposing that "*X* is irreplaceable in *A*'s world" is nonobjective, it does not follow that "*A* is irreplaceable in *A*'s world" is nonobjective. Indeed, it is not. For we know that "*A* is irreplaceable in *A*'s world" is a contradiction, and we know this as the result of having *found it out*. We used simple logical principles to convince ourselves of its inconsistency; it was thus that we found out that the statement was false. Hence it expresses an objective claim.

The reply must be that if *A*'s claim is objective, then *A* is under an obligation to abandon it if it is found out to be false. But I have been saying, in effect, that *A* is under no obligation to abandon his claim. For the discovery that it is false is simply not to the point. *A* did not *assume* that he was irreplaceable, in the hope of carrying out a *reductio ad absurdum* by drawing a self-contradictory conclusion from this assumption. In that case no doubt, and possibly in other cases as well, the discovery of the contradiction in the statement "*A* is irreplaceable in *A*'s world" would be to the point. But instead of *assuming* his own irreplaceability, *A imputed* irreplaceability to himself. This means that he took a position to which facts are irrelevant. To insist that they are always relevant is to deny in a merely dogmatic way the existence of imputations. But surely, a person can refuse to accept a substitute for another person or for a thing regardless of the facts. He can even refuse to accept a substitute for himself. As long as we treat the latter refusal as a refusal and not as in any sense a claim about facts, it is simply an extension of the former refusal. The imputation of irreplaceability is simply a refusal of this kind; it is nothing more than a refusal to accept any substitute.

At the beginning of this chapter I criticized traditional theories of personal identity on the ground that although they arise from a desire to account for the feeling that persons are unique in a way in which things are not, they fail to do justice to this feeling. My contention is that the only analysis that does do justice to it is one in terms of the self-imputation of irreplaceability. It remains to be shown, however, that this analysis meets any *other* requirements that might be imposed on a theory of personal identity. Does it, for example, provide a *criterion* of personal identity? Does it enable one to identify a person as the same person who performed some previous act or existed in a certain place? I now turn to that question.

On my view, persons are self-differentiated; they differentiate themselves from one another. Accordingly, they are self-identified. A person identifies himself in terms of his world, both as its source and as an item in it. It is a world he could not fully share with another without *being* that other; compare "I share Jones's conception of himself as a totality." As self-identifying, the person is normally presumed to be the final authority concerning his own identity. The fact that he can lie about his identity has no tendency to show that he is not the authority. There are occasions, however, when this authority lapses, and we must resort to physical identification. Thus we identify the victim of amnesia by the name-tapes on his clothes and the papers in his wallet. We do not, however, feel that the act of identification has been completed until the authority to identify himself has returned to the patient. Some amnesiacs assume a new personality in place of the lost one. In such cases we tend to go along with the claim that a different person has appeared. If it should turn out that the body of the killer of Martin Luther King, Jr. is divided between two persons, only one of which committed the murder, the law will not hold the other person responsible, but will commit the unfortunate individual to treatment intended to overcome this pathological condition.

The theory of personal identity that I am proposing, then, will differ from the physical theory in its adjudication of particular cases. But the judgments it will make will correspond more closely to our instinctive reactions than will those entailed by the physical theory. The fact is that we do not necessarily equate the identity of a person with that of his body.

Like the memory theory, the view I am putting forward is

nonobjective. But it does not identify a person with anything so transient and full of gaps as consciousness or memory. My world is nothing that I am ever conscious of all at once. It exists as a potentiality, or as a Platonic Form implicit in my experience but never completely exposed to my view.

I know of no way, in fact, to distinguish my intimations of my place in my own world from my conception of myself as a totality. At this juncture it becomes evident that although the imputation of irreplaceability to a thing or person is attitudinal, the self-imputation of irreplaceability expresses more than an attitude. It is rather the awareness of a category or horizon—or, to repeat a phrase, a Platonic Form.

I will conclude this chapter by noting that it supplies additional evidence for a premise used in Chapter 5; namely, that no two persons are the same, so that the expression "the same as X except . . ." is a contradiction whenever X is a person. This assertion clearly amounts to the ascription of a certain kind of uniqueness to each person. It might be supposed, however, that this is an objective uniqueness. However, like the uniqueness that is claimed when a person imputes irreplaceability to something or someone, it is nonobjective. For it is not a *fact* that all persons are different. If it were a fact, we could find it out. But all that we can relevantly find out at the level of generality at which the problem is posed is that whenever we look hard enough, we always see a difference between persons. There is always at least a difference in spatial location. But we have seen that such a difference is trivial in comparison with what we take to be the important differences between persons. Furthermore, the procedure I have just described—that of simply looking until we see what we want to see—is not a way of finding out anything at all. If a statement is empirical rather than analytical or self-contradictory, as the statement that all persons are different allegedly is, we can be said to have found out only if we could have found out the contradictory of what we did find out. Hence we can find out that all persons are different only if the discovery that some are the same was a real possibility. But between any two things we can always see a difference *if we look hard enough*. When we call two things the same, we do not mean that however hard we look we shall never see any differences. We mean only that there is a strong and important similarity. But the procedure to which we commit ourselves when we suppose that it is a *fact* that all persons are different, is totally insensitive to any strong and important similarity.

7 · THE EXPERIENCE OF DEATH AND THE DEATH OF EXPERIENCE

For since by man came death, by man came also the resurrection of the dead.—Cor. 15:21

In Chapter 2, I was careful to point out that not all contradictions are necessary. Many that might seem to evoke the self can easily be eliminated by means of a saving distinction. The self that may have appeared to arise to unify such contradictions is a pseudoself. In this chapter I want to explore the contrast between two contradictions, one of which is necessary and the other not. The unnecessary contradiction is one whose lack of necessity has been displayed by many authors, such as Epicurus, Schopenhauer, Sartre, and Wittgenstein. It is the contradiction into which a person falls in supposing that death is a painful experience. Epicurus's remark that, "Where I am, death is not; where death is, I am not," expresses the saving distinction. I wish to consider in some detail Wittgenstein's presentation of the same distinction. One point that this presentation enables us to see is that often the mere suggestion that a thesis is a contradiction is tantamount to the production of a saving distinction. If calling something a contradiction is sufficient to bring about its withdrawal, the contradiction could hardly have been necessary. Wittgenstein appears to use this strategy.

At *Tractatus* 6.4311, Wittgenstein says[1]

> Death is not an event in life; we do not live to experience death.
> If we take eternity to mean not infinite temporal duration but timelessness, then eternal life belongs to those who live in the present.

1. Ludwig Wittgenstein, *Tractatus Logico-Philosophicus,* translated by D. F. Pears and B. F. McGuinness, London, Routledge & Kegan Paul, 1961. All my references here are to this translation.

Our life has no end in just the way in which our visual field has no limits.

When a philosophical statement is made, there is usually some *particular* point in making it. It is called for as the response to a particular question, problem, doubt, or worry; or it functions to raise a question or arouse a doubt concerning some particular philosophical principle or formulation. In any such case, the statement is specifically addressed to those who raise the question, wrestle with the problem, or are beset by the worry, or espouse the principle in question. A philosophical statement can have a function of this kind even when it is also intended to have quite the different function of contributing to the development of a philosophical system. In this latter case the statement is not specifically addressed to anyone. It is characteristic of philosophical statements, however, that when we do not see to whom in particular they are addressed, we begin to wonder what their justification is; a philosophical statement which there is no *particular* point in making often seems questionable. So the systematic role of a philosophical statement is supported by its dialectical role.

An example is 6.4311. Although this passage undoubtedly contributes to the development of the system of the later part of the *Tractatus,* it also has a dialectical role; it is an argument in response to particular doubts and worries, as well as a series of expository statements. I want to ask: (1) "To whom, precisely, is this argument addressed?" (2) "What, exactly, is the argument?" and (3) "Is this argument valid?"

(1) An argument can hardly be said to be addressed to those who do not accept its premises. For example, if "Death is not an event in life" is a premise of Wittgenstein's argument, the argument cannot be addressed to those for whom death *is* an event in life. (Such people may believe that life continues after death either in a discarnated or reincarnated form.) To a person for whom death *is* an event in life, Wittgenstein's argument will just seem to beg the question. It will appear not as an argument at all, but rather as a series of questionable or pointless assertions. Arguments are addressed to those who do accept their premises. This argument in particular is addressed to those who suppose that death is not an event in life. Such persons are obviously *concerned* about death; the argument is intended to deal with their concern. But *their* concern

about death is only one of several possible concerns about it; and the argument of 6.4311 is not addressed to others of these possible concerns. One who rejected the premise that death is not an event in life might be concerned, for example, about the vicissitudes of an afterlife. But it is not *this* concern with which 6.4311 is intended to deal.

An argument not only is not addressed to those who do not accept its premises, but also it is not addressed to those who already accept its conclusion. To such persons the argument will seem pointless. Hence 6.4311 cannot be addressed to those who already suppose that our life has no end. Of course such persons constitute a subclass of the class of those who believe in an afterlife, and I have just shown that 6.4311 cannot be addressed to any member of this class at all. (As Cebes' question in the *Phaedo*[2] shows, the subclass is not coextensive with the class as a whole; one can believe in an afterlife without believing that life has no end.)

Wittgenstein does have something to say to those who believe in an afterlife, but he says it not in 6.4311 but in 6.4312. Here he attacks the assumption of the eternal survival of the human soul after death, on the ground that "this assumption completely fails to accomplish the purpose for which it has always been intended." The purpose to which Wittgenstein refers here seems to be that of solving a riddle. For he goes on to ask, "Or is some riddle solved by my surviving for ever?" The reason why the assumption of the eternal survival of the human soul after death completely fails to accomplish its purpose is that it merely replaces the riddle it is intended to solve by another riddle: "Is not this eternal life itself as much of a riddle as our present life?"

Wittgenstein's argument in 6.4312 helps us to put the point of 6.4311 more precisely, and to specify its audience more clearly. His criticism at 6.4312 of the assumption of an eternal life is that this assumption fails to come to grips with the riddle of our present life. It does not help us to deal with this riddle. What, then, does help? It seems clear that 6.4311 is intended to help; that remarks such as "Death is not an event in life" and "Our life has no end in just the way in which our visual field has no limits" are addressed precisely to those concerned with the riddle of our present life. We must notice, however, that Wittgenstein is using the word "riddle" (*Rätsel*) in a special sense. In ordinary English a riddle is a kind of question.

2. 86E–88C.

But at 6.5, Wittgenstein makes it clear that the kind of riddle he is concerned with is not a question at all. "The riddle," he says there, "does not exist." But questions do exist; that is, they can be formulated. A riddle, in Wittgenstein's sense, cannot be formulated. It follows that we must not expect 6.4311 to answer a question. But if it is addressed to those who are concerned with a riddle, it ought in some way to come to grips with that riddle; it ought to *mitigate* it.

If a riddle is not a question, what is it? It is a source of concern; it is something we can be *bothered* about, without being quite able to put the concern or bother into words. Our present life is a riddle partly because we are anxious about death, even though we would find it difficult to formulate our anxiety. This anxiety, to which 6.4311 is addressed, should be contrasted with other anxieties about death, one of which I have already mentioned. Those who worry about the vicissitudes of the afterlife do not face a riddle, for they can readily communicate their worries. If what concerns a man is his chances of getting into Heaven or of being suitably embodied in the next reincarnation, someone with the expertise of a priest could not only understand his questions but even offer an answer to them. Indeed, it is an entertainable hypothesis (put forward by d'Holbach among others) that it was the priest who induced the worrier to worry in the first place.

Another concern about death with which the anxiety addressed by 6.4311 ought to be contrasted is the puzzle *whether* there is an afterlife or not. But this puzzle is a formulable question, and it is in 6.4312 that Wittgenstein attempts to answer it in the negative. He speaks of the eternal survival of the human soul as an "assumption," and dismisses this assumption as not accomplishing the purpose for which it was intended. The audience to which 6.4311 is addressed is thus restricted to people who have already reached the conclusion that there is no afterlife. But it is restricted in further ways as well, for it is addressed only to those *anxious* about there being no afterlife. Notice that there must furthermore be a *connection* between the anxiety and the disbelief. A disbeliever in the afterlife might be anxious about the welfare of his survivors on the ground that after he died there would be no one left to care for them, but 6.4311 is not addressed to him, since it is not his disbelief as such that makes him anxious.

What, then, *is* a member of the audience of 6.4311 anxious about? Almost all that can be said on this point is that such persons worry about death because they shrink from the prospect of ceasing to be. The contention that little or nothing more can be said about the content of this worry is supported by the difficulty of communicating the worry itself. I have already pointed out that a person worried about the vicissitudes of an afterlife, or one puzzled about *whether* there is an afterlife or not, can communicate his worry; he can formulate it as a question. But if you are simply worried about the prospect of ceasing to be, how can you formulate your worry? All that you say is that you do not want to cease to be. But if your interlocutor is a person who is *not* worried about ceasing to be, you will not have succeeded in explaining your worry to him. It will remain a mystery to him why you are worried at all. A worry which in this way remains a mystery is a riddle; because it is not a question, it cannot be answered, but perhaps it can somehow be mitigated. Whether it can remains to be seen.

(2) How *does* Wittgenstein attempt to mitigate the riddle? What is his argument? The strongest clue is provided by the third sentence of 6.4311, "Our life has no end in just the way in which our visual field has no limits." That is to say, our life has no limit that it could encounter; we do not live to experience death. This thesis about limits crops up, of course, elsewhere in the *Tractatus*. In the Preface, Wittgenstein says, "In order to be able to set a limit to thought, we should have to find both sides of the limit thinkable (i.e., we should have to be able to think what cannot be thought.)" According to this statement, the attempt to set a thinkable limit to thought is self-contradictory. It follows that if anyone believed that thought had a thinkable limit, and worried as a result of that belief, the worry could be assuaged by pointing out that the belief is self-contradictory.

Similarly, in order to be able to set a visible limit to our visual field, we should have to find both sides of the limit visible (that is, we should have to be able to see what cannot be seen). And in order to be able to set an experienceable limit to our experience, we should have to find both sides of the limit experienceable (that is, we should have to be able to experience what cannot be experienced). Thus we do not live to experience death. Death is not an event in life.

I conclude, then, that 6.4311 attempts to mitigate the riddle to which it is addressed by pointing out that the riddle presupposes a contradiction. The very idea that there be an experience of death is self-contradictory. Wittgenstein dissolves the contradiction by saying that if there is a limit to experience, it is unexperienceable, and so not worth worrying about.

(3) Is the argument valid? That is, does 6.4311 succeed in mitigating the riddle to which it is addressed? Is the contradiction it dissolves the very one into which the worrier has fallen? It seems clear that it need not be, for consider someone worried not about the experience of death, but about the death of experience. What worries him is not the prospect of experiencing the limit to experience, but just that there should be a limit to experience at all. He is upset by the horrible thought that experience may not be endless, in the sense that at any given moment more is to come. It does not help him to be told that experience *is* endless—in another sense. Thus Wittgenstein's argument leaves a gap between the alleged worry it assuages and what actually concerns the audience it addresses—or at least some members of the audience.

The gap is also revealed by the following parody of the passage from the *Tractatus* under discussion.

> The act of falling asleep is not an event in our waking life; we are not awake when this event occurs.
> If we take eternity to mean not infinite temporal duration but timelessness, then eternal insomnia belongs to those who are awake in the present.
> Our waking life has no end in just the way in which our visual field has no limits.

All that I have done in order to produce this parody is to substitute the idea of sleep for that of death, and that of being awake for that of living. Obviously, the parody is as true as the original: everything that Wittgenstein says of death would equally well apply to sleep.[3] But aside from the fact that a person might worry about falling asleep while driving or while in church, no one is worried over sleep. Certainly, no one is worried over it in the way that people are often worried over death. It follows that what worries people about death is something that Wittgenstein has *not* said about it—something that would not apply equally to sleep. This feature is obviously the irreversibility of death. Although we normally awake from sleep, we do not recover consciousness after dying—or at least such might well be the belief of those who are anxious about death.

3. Of course there are cases in which the sleeper is conscious of being asleep, but such cases do not concern me here.

So far I have argued that the contradiction pointed out by Wittgenstein—the contradiction inherent in supposing that one could experience one's own death—is not one into which the worried people whom Wittgenstein is addressing have necessarily fallen. And if they have fallen into this contradiction, they are easily extricated from it. My conclusion, then, is that Wittgenstein does not succeed in meeting the point of everyone comprising the audience he addresses in 6.4311. Perhaps it will be objected that what this conclusion really shows is that he was not really addressing these people in the first place. But if we generalize the principle of this objection, we are led to an odd result; namely, that any philosophical argument must meet the point of everyone it addresses. It would follow that every philosophical argument must be valid!

Another clear-cut example of a philosophical argument that does not meet the point of the audience it addresses is found in 6.4312. This paragraph is addressed to people who believe in the eternal survival of the human soul after death. Its punch line is "Is not this eternal life itself as much of a riddle as our present life?" But one may wonder whether this *ad hominem* question really makes its point. Wittgenstein seems to be arguing that *because* an eternal life is itself a riddle, it cannot be appealed to in order to solve the riddle of our present life. But surely an eternal life is not a riddle *in the way in which* our present life is a riddle. The riddle of our present life—at least, the riddle that concerns Wittgenstein in this particular paragraph—arises from the fact that we must die. But an *eternal* life is precisely one in which we will not die. Hence the assumption of an eternal life does go at least some distance toward meeting the needs posed by the riddle of our present life. Of course, an eternal life is also a riddle; for we do not know what the purpose of such a life could be. In exactly the same way, our present life is a riddle; for we can have no idea of what *its* ultimate purposes are —why we are here on earth. It is not because our present life is a riddle *in this way* that we assume an eternal life. We assume an eternal life only in the effort to solve *another* riddle—namely, the one dealt with at 6.4311—and Wittgenstein's remarks at 6.4312 have no tendency to show that an eternal life does not solve *that* riddle. In dismissing the "assumption" of an eternal life, in fact, he is dismissing the only thesis that could possibly be of any help to those whom he unsuccessfully addresses in 6.4311.

Wittgenstein's very argument at 6.4311 calls our attention to the existence of people whose worry over the prospect of death is more than just a transient contradiction into which they have fallen in a moment of inattentiveness. It is not the experience of death that worries these people whom Wittgenstein's argument fails to touch, but the death of experience—a state in which one's final experience has occurred and in which one is to remain unconscious forever after. I will argue, however, that no one can consistently form the idea of such a state. The worry is an unmitigable contradiction.

In his article on "My Death" in the Macmillan *Encyclopedia of Philosophy*,[4] Paul Edwards argues that there is nothing to prevent a person from forming the idea of his own death just as he forms the idea of the death of another person. Although it is true that I must be alive to form the idea of my death, my being alive is not part of the content of the idea itself. Accordingly, my death is not something I cannot imagine in a perfectly straightforward way. I agree with Edwards that a person who imagines his own death need not picture himself as alive. But a person imagining his own death in the manner described by Edwards need not be envisaging the permanent cessation of experience anticipated by some of those whom Wittgenstein addresses, and hence is not necessarily facing the real problem. If I take the imaginary role of spectator of my own corpse, I may do so in the belief that in another form I am to continue my life. As I have attempted to suggest, however, this is not the only idea a person can form of his own death. And its logical innocuousness does not imply the logical innocuousness of all such ideas. The idea of the permanent cessation of experience, for example, poses difficulties of a different order from those involved in the presupposition that the spectator of an event must be alive.

To be sure, Edwards says that "a person thinking of his own death is thinking of the destruction or disintegration of his body *and of the cessation of his experiences*."[5] And it is clearly true that I can imagine myself stretched out on the mortuary table, my life over, *my experiences completed*. The fact that I must be alive to imagine this scene does not in any way enter into the scene itself. In this act of imagination, however, I see myself in just the way that I see another person. Exactly as I would argue from the premise that another is stretched out on the mortuary table to the conclusion that his experience had ended, so I now argue from my own similar situa-

4. Vol. 5, pp. 416–19.
5. *Ibid.*, p. 416; italics mine.

tion to the conclusion that my experience has come to an end. And my reaching this conclusion is not in any way hampered by the fact that I must be alive to reach it. Yet it seems clear that a person claiming to be concerned over the permanent cessation of his experience need not be thinking of it in this roundabout way. Instead of thinking of his body and making inferences regarding his experience, he may be thinking directly of his experience itself. It is here that trouble arises. For from this point of view, within experience itself, I cannot imagine the final cessation of my experience. What, after all, would that be like? It would be like having the experience of a stick or stone. Try as hard as I may, this is a possibility I cannot fathom. Yet it is precisely the idea of my own death.

It might be objected that one can easily form the idea of an experience after which I am to have no further experience. But what is it like for an experience to be final? Can its finality be asserted except from the point of view of some succeeding experience? If I were trying to imagine my final experience, how would I go about imagining its finality?

The conclusion seems inescapable that some people—the ones to whom Wittgenstein's argument is addressed but who remain unimpressed by this argument—have formed a self-contradictory idea of their own death. They have imagined the unimaginable. Nor is it of the slightest use to point out to such persons that they contradict themselves. This remark betrays a lack of understanding of their position; it does not take that position seriously. If I am in trouble and know it, you are not being much of a help if you merely tell me that I am in trouble.

One further remark can be made in passing about Edwards' article. He comments that people who have trouble with "my death" seem to be unconcerned about the idea of the nonexistence of the person before birth. This is a perceptive point; to precisely the extent that there is a paradox of death, there must also be a paradox of birth. "I might not have been born" expresses a difficulty similar to that expressed by "I may die." Instead of arguing by *modus tollens,* as Edwards does, that the paradox of death is a will-o'-the-wisp, we can argue, as I have in effect already argued in Chapter 5, that there is a real and urgent paradox of birth.

In speaking of death as an "unrealizable,"[6] Sartre showed that he grasped the point I have been making. An unrealizable is anything

6. *Being and Nothingness,* translated by Hazel E. Barnes, New York, Philosophical Library, 1956, p. 547.

that makes consciousness aware that it has an *outside*. It is a limit to consciousness that one cannot be conscious of, because all consciousness takes place inside the limit. Yet, precisely because it is beyond consciousness, it casts its shadow on conciousness. It is a perpetual exteriority which exists to be interiorized.[7] Wittgenstein's reference to an "eternal life" in the present is the confession of a man on whose consciousness the limits cast no shadows.

Sartre's advice is that each of us should regard his own impending death as an ultimate absurdity. It is clear that he means to contrast this absurdity with concerns that are not absurd. Yet it is odd that a man for whom consciousness is through and through self-contradictory ("It is what it is not and it is not what it is"[8]) should be bothered by this particular contradiction.

My own conclusion is that the idea of the permanent cessation of my own experience is in fact a contradiction, and one for which there is no saving distinction. The point is analogous to one that I argued in the last chapter. If I think of myself in relation to my own world, I face a contradiction. I cannot stand outside my world to see whether I am replaceable or irreplaceable in it; for wherever I stand, I am in my world. Similarly, I cannot stand outside my experience to see whether it continues or comes to an end; for wherever I stand, I am inside my own experience, even if the act of standing is but an act of imagination. The idea of my death is thus structurally similar to the act of referring to myself by pointing to myself. And just as it is necessary for me on at least some occasions to refer to myself, either by pointing or in some other paradoxical way, so it is necessary for me sometimes to envisage the permanent cessation of my experience.

The self, or at least the soul, has traditionally had a role to play in connection with reflections on death. As the vehicle of personal survival of death, it has come into existence as a way of dealing with our worries over death. In my own view, too, the self can arise from these worries. But when it does, its function is not to assuage the worries, or even to answer a question. Its function is rather just to bring the worries into focus—to provide a *pou sto* from which they can be resolutely faced, rather than schizophrenically avoided or loaded onto the soul to be borne away.

7. *Ibid.*, p. 529.
8. *Ibid.*, p. 58.

8 · SELF, CONSCIOUSNESS, AND SELF-CONSCIOUSNESS

Every act of cognition must refer to an object other than itself, and therefore no act of cognition can be aware of itself.—John Laird

From the consideration that a person is a subject, that he is conscious of the world and of himself, the conclusion has traditionally been drawn that the self exists as an essential requirement of such subjectivity or consciousness. Tradition has held the self to be related to consciousness in various ways. The fact that one can be conscious of himself has sometimes been taken to mean that there is a self of which, in moments of intimate reflection, one can be conscious. It has alternatively been taken to mean that there is a self in the form of a transcendental ego, a subject that engages in intimate reflections without itself ever being an object on which reflection is possible. Again, it has been argued that the self is the unity of consciousness or experience. I will begin by briefly criticizing each of these views. My purpose, however, is not merely polemical. I want to propose a different view of the relation between self and subjectivity or consciousness, a view that seems to me inherently more satisfactory than any of those it displaces.

I turn to the view that in self-consciousness one can be conscious of a self. This view seems to pivot on a solecism. In the ordinary use of the term "self-conscious" to characterize the awkward comportment of one who is shy, it means simply a heightened consciousness of one's own behavior. In more technical contexts, self-consciousness means consciousness of consciousness; there may be a problem about the possibility of this reflexive relation, but there is not any intention to refer to a self. To suppose that one can be conscious of a self as one is conscious of other objects is simply to refuse to exercise the care that Hume exercised in examining the possible objects of consciousness—care illustrated by the following celebrated passage:

> There are some philosophers who imagine that we are every moment intimately conscious of what we call our *self*; that we feel its existence. . . . For my part, when I enter most intimately into what I call *myself* I always stumble on some particular perception or other. . . . Were all my perceptions removed, could I neither think, nor feel, nor see, nor love, nor hate . . . I should be entirely annihilated. . . . If anyone thinks he has a different notion of *himself*, I must confess I can reason no longer with him . . . he may perhaps perceive something simple and continued which he calls *himself*, though I am certain there is no such principle in me. But, setting aside some metaphysicians of this kind, I may venture to affirm of the rest of mankind that they are nothing but a bundle or collection of different perceptions which succeed each other. . . . The mind is a kind of theatre where perceptions make their appearance, mingle, and glide away. . . . There is no simplicity and no identity whatever natural propension we may have to imagine that simplicity and identity. The comparison to the theatre must not mislead us; the successive perceptions themselves constitute the mind. . . .[1]

Notice that consciousness itself does not turn up as one of the objects of consciousness in Hume's account. I shall argue that consciousness of consciousness is in fact a contradiction, and that from the acceptance of this contradiction a self arises. But this is not at all the same as saying that self-consciousness is consciousness of a self.

There are thinkers, of course, who have performed Hume's introspective exercise without obtaining his negative results. Bergson and Whitehead claimed to have encountered a self in intimate reflection. But what they encountered was not what Hume failed to encounter. As Nathan Rotenstreich points out, "Whitehead was impressed by Hume's criticism of the identity of the self; he thought to overcome this criticism by yielding to the main point of Hume, that is to say, to the view that the subject is not self-identical, but perpetually emerging from the data."[2] But a self that does not maintain its identity can hardly perform the other services traditionally required of it; for example, it cannot serve as a locus of

1. *A Treatise of Human Nature*, Bk. I, Sect. VI.
2. *On the Human Subject, Studies in the Phenomenology of Ethics and Politics*, Springfield, Illinois, Charles C Thomas, 1966, p. 27.

responsibility. It is an unsatisfactory replacement for the self disavowed by Hume.

In speaking of the mind as "a kind of theatre," Hume, his disclaimer to the contrary notwithstanding, is already approaching the second view of the relation between consciousness and the self, according to which the self is a transcendental ego. This view is, of course, developed by Kant and Husserl. It rests on the assumption that the idea of a subject that is an object to itself is a contradiction. If it is also assumed that there is a subject, the conclusion is that this subject can never be an object. Such an account would explain why Hume failed to find the subject of his own experiences. It was present in the effort, but present as the very agent of the effort rather than as the goal.

I have already suggested my agreement with the assumption that it is self-contradictory to suppose that a subject can be an object to itself. The principle that serves as the motto of this chapter lies at the heart of the nature of cognition. And cognition in its more general acceptation is synonymous with consciousness, since to cognize is simply to be conscious of. Consciousness is furthermore isomorphic with the act of referring to something by pointing to it. The incapacity of consciousness to be its own object is structurally identical with the incapacity of the pointing needle to point to itself. Consciousness of consciousness is a contradiction.

A transcendental ego posited merely as a way of avoiding this contradiction, however, seems to me the product of an overreaction. One indication of the excess is that the contradiction is avoided in this way only at the expense of an infinite regress; because no subject can be object to itself, when we want to treat a subject as an object, we must posit a further subject to which it is an object. Another indication is that the transcendental ego that results is defined only negatively; it is a self by default, posited only to avoid a contradiction. It is totally devoid of content. It lacks both the intimacy and the individuality traditionally associated with the self.

My own view is that the proper reaction is to grasp the nettle rather than backing away from it. I will have more to say on this later. For the moment it is sufficient to note that in the case of pointing we do grasp the nettle whenever we accept with equanimity the report that someone has succeeded in referring to himself by pointing to himself.

The view that the self is the unity of consciousness is also

Kantian and Husserlian. My objection to it is that the unity of consciousness need not in fact be attributed to anything beyond consciousness itself. For it is the very nature of consciousness to unify itself. Consider temporal unity. We may contrast a series of states of consciousness with a batch of loose pages, some of which I know to belong to a diary. The pages do not unify *themselves,* but *I* can unify them by arranging those with explicit or inferrible dates according to their temporal order and discarding the pages that I decide do not belong. But the idea that the "pages" of consciousness might have to be arranged by an external unifier just does not make sense. If there is any doubt as to the order of the states, it is my consciousness itself that both raises and dispels the doubt. Any given state already presupposes one ordering or another of the previous ones. Also, as is not the case with the pages, there could not be any state that does not belong to the consciousness in question; there is nothing to be discarded. For any state of which I am conscious belongs *ipso facto* to my consciousness. Hence I cannot review states of consciousness with a view to deciding whether they are mine or someone else's.[3]

Before presenting my own view of the relation between self and consciousness, I should indicate more fully what I take to be the nature of consciousness. There are many modes of consciousness; we can be conscious of physical things, of other persons, of our own thoughts, of aesthetic qualities, and of moral principles. In the broad sense in which I am using the term we can even be conscious of our own dreams. What is common to all these cases is a distance interposed between the subject and what he is conscious of. A subject completely immersed in experience would not be conscious of it. It is a platitude that we are indeed unconscious of most of the background noises, pressures, luminosities, odors, and visceral sensations that impinge upon us at any given moment. We are unaware of them not because they are remote but because they are too near. There is no distance between us and them.

The question whether machines can be conscious has many ramifications, but it seems clear that present-day machines are not in any event conscious of what we say we "communicate" to them. We typically communicate with machines by means of punched

3. An incisive statement of the reasons why the hypothesis of self or ego is not required to account for the unity of consciousness can be found in A. Gurwitsch, "A Non-egological Conception of Consciousness," *Philosophy and Phenomenological Research,* Vol. I, 1941, pp. 328–329.

cards. The cards are sensed by a device that translates the holes in them to electrical pulses; and these pulses then energize the devices (for example, magnets) which "store" the data. But at no point in the process is there any distance. The machine is immersed in the cards fed to it just as a person is immersed in his background environment. In order to see what more would be required for consciousness to arise, contrast a malfunction which prevents the machine from correctly storing a datum fed to it, with a person's misinterpretation of something he is conscious of. What in the person would correspond to the machine's malfunction is some deformation of a sense organ, causing him, for example, to see red as brown, just as the malfunctioning machine interprets a comma as a slash. But a person can misinterpret his data in a different way as well. He can mis-see a tree as a man. This mistake may have nothing to do with the condition of his sense organs. It arises only because the distance that separates him from the datum—and here I obviously do not mean merely physical distance—presents him with the choice of interpreting the datum as a tree or as a man. Consciousness, even in its most rudimentary form, is always characterized by such a choice. I am not conscious at all of the bright light that confronts me as I awaken from a postoperative sleep until I am forced with the need to see it as one thing or another. Thus consciousness presupposes the possibility of misinterpretation. But the success of the machine does not presuppose the possibility of malfunctioning.

Another way of putting the point is to say that consciousness presupposes self-consciousness. The very notion of being conscious of something without being *aware* that one is conscious of it is incoherent. I refer again to the experience of the postoperative patient who becomes aware that a bright light has been before him. Before he achieves this awareness—this consciousness of being conscious—he cannot be said to be conscious of the bright light at all. By "being aware" I do not of course mean knowing in any explicit way. A person can see something which he does not until later realize he has seen. He was conscious of the thing, and hence aware of being conscious of it; but he did not *know* that he saw it, in the sense of being able explicitly to formulate what he saw, or to report or reflect upon it. In Sartrean terms, his consciousness was "non-thetic."

The question whether a machine can be conscious can be

answered again in terms of the present discussion. No doubt machines can respond to stimuli of many sorts. They can also respond to their own responses to stimuli. But since the response to the response to a stimulus cannot be *identical* with the very response to the stimulus, consciousness cannot be achieved by a machine. But it is definitive of my consciousness of anything that it be *identical* with my consciousness of my consciousness of it.

My point can also be expressed by saying that in the first place, a person can be conscious of something only if a wedge has been inserted between him and it. In the next chapter I will develop the theme that rhetoric is the art of driving this wedge. (I will also argue that a person can be the audience of his own rhetoric.) In the second place, the wedge is not effective unless the person is conscious of *it*. To be conscious, he must not only occupy a position at a distance from the object but must also be aware of the distance. He must not only *be* other than the object but *know* that he is other than it. Since the computer is not *aware* of being other than the deck of punched cards fed to it, it *is* not other; the inputting of the deck is part of the continuous train of events that *constitutes* the operation of the machine.

Of course, if intended as an explicit definition of "consciousness," this characterization is defective, because it immediately gives rise to an infinite regress. One can be conscious of something only if one is conscious of the wedge between him and it; one can be conscious of the wedge only if one is conscious of the wedge between him and it. But my characterization of consciousness is not meant to be a definition. Like "Person," "Consciousness" is one of the primitive terms in this book; it is "logically primitive," to use Strawson's expression. In addition, I have already indicated how I am inclined to deal with an infinite regress of this sort. In the case of the needle pointing to the needle pointing to the needle . . . I argued in Chapter 4 that we could avoid the regress if we were only willing to accept a contradiction. The regress is then replaced by the person envisaged as standing outside himself and pointing at himself. In the present situation the regress can similarly be replaced by an outright contradiction. Consciousness is always of something other than itself—here is where the factor of distance enters. But consciousness is always of itself—this is what it means to say that the distance does not exist unless we are aware of it.

Perhaps "Subjectivity" expresses better than "Consciousness" the contradiction I have been attempting to characterize. The objective by definition contains no contradictions. Hence when one occurs it must be assigned to subjectivity. It is to subjectivity that all errors are ascribed. In the objective world there are no errors; to err is human. The obverse side of this is that the objective world contains no correct statements, either. Truth and falsity are not properties discoverable within this world, but rather are expressions of claims made by subjective beings. There is an analogy between these claims and the awareness that one is conscious. Just as I cannot be conscious of the bright light without being aware that I am conscious of it, so I cannot discover anything about the objective world without at least implicitly claiming that my report of my discovery is true. Unless I know that I know, I do not know at all. In my subjectivity I must stand both in the objective world and outside it.

I am in a position now to deal with an objection that might be urged against my previous discussion of the unity of consciousness. I said that any state of which I am conscious belongs *ipso facto* to my consciousness. But does not the use of "my" presuppose a principle of unification more ultimate than consciousness itself? This would contradict the claim that consciousness unifies itself. In particular, it might appear that a transcendent self—a "my" attaching to every state of consciousness—is the principle of unification. But I want to argue that no such ego *antedates* the unification of consciousness. From consciousness and its inconsistent fusion with self-consciousness a self arises. It is this self that claims ownership of the consciousness out of the ecstasis of which it arises, and thus makes possible the use of expressions like "my consciousness." Consciousness is not unified by an antecedent sense of ownership, for the "my" arises at the same time as consciousness itself. In complete immersion in experience there is no sense of ownership—when I am totally absorbed in a task or in a reverie I am not aware of *my* absorption. The identification of a state of consciousness as *mine* is in fact tantamount to the identification of a state of consciousness *tout simple*—to say that it is mine is no more than to say that it has been identified; that is, noticed or caught, and hence thrown outside itself. But this condition in which it is thrown outside itself is simply its ecstasis; that is, the unification of the poles of the contradiction of self-consciousness.

"My" is, of course, the genitive of "I," and in view of the way in which I have been associating "my" with a self, it might be thought that I take the position that "I" simply denotes a self. But this position is, as I have argued before, untenable. "I" denotes a person, not a self, if it denotes anything. "I go to town" means "Johnstone goes to town," not "Johnstone's self goes to town." It is clear enough, however, that "I" and "my" *presuppose* a self; they can be spoken or thought only by persons, as I have argued in Chapter 4.

It remains to discuss briefly a kind of consciousness that has been regarded as having a particularly important role in connection with the self. I am alluding to memory. Certainly memory plays a part in my identification of myself. An amnesiac is unable to identify himself because he has forgotten who he is. But perhaps the amnesiac's loss is not precisely a loss of memory, or at least not entirely that.[4] I know that I am Johnstone, and I know this without inferring it from any premises. But must this noninferential knowledge be described as memory? Do I *remember* who I am? If knowing who I am were the same as knowing my own name, it could be regarded as an act of memory. To know the name of this wildflower is not to have forgotten it. But in order to know who I am, I need to know more than my name. An amnesiac can find his name on the name tape sewn into his jacket but still not know his own identity. The failure is not of memory but of recognition. If I have forgotten everything, it is unlikely that I shall be able to recognize myself, but this is a limiting case. Certainly I do not need to remember very much in order to know who I am. For example, I can wake up in a strange place without having any idea how I got there and still experience no difficulty in recognizing myself.

The possibility of not recognizing oneself, as in amnesia, is one further piece of evidence, if any were needed, that a person's relationships to himself are fundamentally the same as those that he bears to other persons. Just as one may either misrecognize or altogether fail to recognize another person, so one may misrecognize oneself (witness Smith who thinks he is Napoleon), or totally fail to recognize oneself, even to the point that one does not even know his own sex. In *A Clergyman's Daughter,* Orwell writes of a young woman awakening to a profound amnesia:

Who was she? She turned the question over in her mind, and

4. The polemical thrust of these remarks is against Shoemaker. See especially *Self-knowledge and Self-identity,* Chapter 4.

found that she had not the dimmest notion of who she was; except that, watching the people and horses passing, she grasped that she was a human being and not a horse. And at that the question altered itself and took this form: "Am I a man or a woman?" Again neither feeling nor memory gave her any clue to the answer. But at that moment, by accident possibly, her fingertips brushed against her body. She realized more clearly than before that her body existed, and that it was her own—that it was, in fact, herself. She began to explore it with her hands, and her hands encountered breasts. She was a woman, therefore. Only women had breasts.[5]

Dorothy Hare's failure to recognize herself, recounted in this quotation, shows that a person can be just as incompetent in identifying himself as he can be in identifying another. It suggests another point worth making, too—that there is no reason in principle why a person should achieve greater competence in *characterizing* himself more than he has in *characterizing* others. But it has a further ramification more germane to our present topic of memory. This is that the self cannot be defined as the thread of memory. Thinkers like Bergson and Whitehead have attempted to define it in this way. By "self," I take it, they have meant at least a locus of inquiry. But Dorothy's inquiry into her own identity presupposes an inquirer *not* defined through memory. Of course we do not need a case as extreme as hers in order to make this point. I have already reminded my readers that consciousness orders its own contents. It is not my *memories* that determine *me* but rather it is *I* who determine my *memories*—I can not only determine their proper order but even decide whether they are really memories or not.

Having attacked one account of how the self is related to its memories, I want to propose another such account. I want to argue that the self arises not as the thread of its memories but as the ecstasis of them. (Hence ecstasis, as I shall be referring to it, individuates, in contrast to traditional versions of ecstasis which dissolve individuation.) I shall begin my argument by asking whether there is any kind of memory into which the self does not enter at all. It might seem that in pure reminiscing this condition is met. There may indeed be a kind of reminiscing in which a person is so wholly absorbed in the past that there is no occasion for the appearance of the self. But to the extent that the reminiscing is a witnessing of the past rather than a total absorption in

5. George Orwell, *A Clergyman's Daughter*, New York, Avon Books, n.d., p. 69.

it, it must evoke the self in just the way that any other occasion of consciousness evokes it. The contrast between the position of the subject and that of the object is self-contradictory, and the contradiction generates a self which is at the same time required to juxtapose the poles of the contradiction.

There is, of course, a more deliberate act of recollecting past episodes as well; and memory of this kind has its own ecstasis—one that philosophers have been attempting to evade for hundreds of years. This is the contradiction in claiming that a datum is both past and present. One attempted route of evasion is to suppose that actually a present datum is a *sign* of a past episode. But surely a memory is more than a sign. The hole made by a bullet is a sign of a past shot, but not a memory of a past shot, and unless there were memories of past episodes, we could have no idea of the past at all. We cannot generate this idea, furthermore, in terms of signs alone. To put the argument differently: it makes sense to call A a sign of B only when A and B can be compresent. But the memory image and the past episode are compresent only if the memory image is itself past. Yet it must also be present. One can only conclude that memory is a fundamental ecstasis—a situation in which I stand outside myself to occupy both the present and the past. For in the act of remembering a past scene I encounter myself as both present and past. This is the truth that has been distorted into the theory that the self *is* the thread of memory.

Not only is the ecstasis of memory evocative of the self, but also the ecstasis *presupposes* a self. For unless I am willing to stand in both the past and present, I shall recollect nothing. Either I shall be indulging in a pure reverie of reminiscence, in which I select no particular content for present examination, or I shall be wholly preoccupied with the present. Computers are sometimes spoken of as having memories, but the trend nowadays is toward the use of the term "core" rather than "memory"; it is as if the designers and operators had become aware that in speaking of "memory" they were indulging in a flight of fancy. The reason why a computer does not in fact have a memory is that it can deal only with available data—"bits," as they are called. Whether a bit was stored one microsecond or ten minutes ago does not make any difference to the way in which it is used in the computation into which it enters. There is no way in which the machine could take account of this difference except by attaching different subscripts to the early bit and the late bit, in which case it would be dealing with two bits, not one—and dealing with them both in the present. The remarks I have just made apply in an obvious way to memory traces in the human brain. In terms of them, we can account for the storage of past events, but not for the appreciation of these events as past. Such appreciation requires a person to assign the image called up in the present by a memory trace to the past, and this assignment is always the acceptance of a contradiction.

9 · RHETORIC, INTERFACE, AND THE OTHER

Properly speaking, neither the other Ego himself, nor his subjective processes or his appearances themselves, nor anything else belonging to his own essence, becomes given in our experience originally. If it were, if what belongs to the other's own essence were directly accessible, it would be merely a moment of my own essence, and ultimately he himself and I myself would be the same.—Husserl

A traditional context for the discussion of the self is the problem of other minds. This problem rests on the assumption that a person has a privileged access to at least some of his own mental states. It is privileged in the sense that others do not share it. Only he, for example, knows in a direct way that he has a headache. Others know it only indirectly. One ramification of the problem is to account for this indirect knowledge in such a way that it can still be properly called knowledge at all. Failing direct evidence, what evidence of any kind is there? Another ramification is to maintain the distinction between mental states to which access is privileged and others to which it may not be. Are not all mental states ultimately on a par with headaches? We seem powerless to avoid reaching the conclusion that no knowledge of another's mental states is possible. What is it, then that even leads us to suppose that he *has* mental states? As skepticism of this sort develops, the concept of the self as the locus of privileged access has often arisen as its counterpart. So conceived, it is the solipsistic subject, for whom there are no other persons, only the appearances of persons.

My own view of the way in which the self is involved in the problem of the other minds is predictably different from this. My view, briefly, is that the self emerges precisely because there is a problem. In emerging, it authenticates the problem. According to the solipsistic position I have just sketched, on the other hand, the self in emerging abolishes the problem. For if solipsism is true, other minds no longer constitute a challenge to our powers of knowing, since they do not even exist.

In addition to making this pronouncement, I want to propose a more specific approach to the problem of other minds, an approach that makes use of some of the conclusions of Chapter 8. There I considered whether a machine can be conscious of what we are said to "communicate" to it. Since communication is possible only if there are other minds, it is useful to see if we can establish that there are cases in which we would say that communication genuinely occurs. (My argument here is thus an appeal to circumspect usage, not to any alleged fact about communication.) One way of establishing this point is to show that a distinction can be made between what we might be tempted to suppose that we communicate to a machine, and what we actually do communicate to ourselves as well as to others. We shall find that the fact that we can communicate with ourselves shows that even within a single person there are "other minds" to be addressed. Once we have reached this conclusion, the transition to other minds in other persons is not hard to make.

Communication is often contrasted with rhetoric. The former is alleged to transmit propositions and the latter attitudes. Beginning with this contrast as a first approximation, I want to show that communication, in fact, always requires rhetoric. It is this property that enables us to distinguish genuine from specious communication, and hence to establish the existence of genuine communication, and, by implication, that of other minds.

Is it possible to envisage a situation in which rhetoric has been totally suppressed in favor of pure communication? In such a situation there would be no need for persuasion. Information would replace argument. Instead of attempting to convince me of the truth of a certain proposition or the correctness of a certain course of action, my interlocutor would simply tell me. My readers may feel that this situation is already familiar to them, in the writings of Orwell if not in accounts of past and existing monolithic states. But these are not situations without rhetoric; they are rather situations which ironically must be sustained by rhetoric. Only through the official rhetoric can private and deviant uses of rhetoric be rigorously suppressed. A situation totally devoid of rhetoric would be more appropriately exemplified by a system of devices designed to receive, store, manipulate, and transmit information. Certainly rhetoric could have no effect on such a system. One cannot argue with a machine—one can only control it. The question I want to ask is whether a machine of this kind (or a system of them) does in fact represent a situation in which we have succeeded in suppressing rhetoric in favor of communication alone.

Consider a deck of punched cards constituting a computer program. It might be supposed that no more perfect vehicle of communication could be imagined. There is no ambiguity whatever about the information conveyed to the machine. Nor would it make sense to suppose the machine to be in any way reluctant to receive the information. A rhetoric of belief would be absolutely gratuitous even if it were possible. Nor is there any need for a rhetoric of action. Some of the cards in the deck formulate commands to the machine. For example, if a certain statement is true, the machine is told to go to another statement designated as "200" and execute the command therein expressed; otherwise, it is to go to "300." The machine does not need to be convinced of the correctness of this course of action. Indeed, the very notion that a course of action would be correct or incorrect for it is tenuous, to say the least.

Using a deck of punched cards, or some other input device such as a magnetic tape or a light pen, I establish absolute communication with the computer. Is it not obvious, though, that this absolute communication is identical with absolute noncommunication? I "tell" the computer that the initial value of the variable N is 15. But have I really communicated anything to it? It has no choice but to accept 15 as the value of N. Perfect communication, and hence noncommunication, characterizes the transmission of messages from man to the machine and from the machine to other machines.[1] In order to show why it amounts to noncommunication, let us contrast it with the transmission of a message from machine to man. Suppose that "N = 15" is not the initial datum of a problem, but rather the solution to a problem that a user has programmed a computer to solve. Accordingly, the user in question will receive from the machine a

---

1. In Chapter 1, I proposed taking the computer programmer seriously when he spoke of what the machine "knew." Why am I not taking him seriously when he speaks of "communicating to the machine"? The answer is that I was playing devil's advocate in Chapter 1, assuming, with my hypothetical antagonist, that the machine knew, and showing that even if it did know it could not know the right and do the wrong. Here, on the other hand, my polemical purpose requires me to take an official stand on computer–center talk. If anyone wants to apply that stand to Chapter 1, let him simply delete the pages concerned with the first sense in which a computer can be said to "know."

sheet of paper on which is printed the expression "N = 15". One might suppose that this, too, is perfect communication. Certainly there is no ambiguity about it. But the fact remains that the user need not accept it. He may say, "Hey! Wait a minute! That can't be right!" Computers do not always tell the truth; they do so only when they are correctly programmed and given data that are correct; even if "N = 15" is actually the correct answer, the user need not accept it, for his past dealings with the machine may have made a doubting Thomas of him. And even if the user does not reject "N = 15" as the solution to the problem, he need not accept it either. His mind may simply be on something else. Perfect communication presupposes a perfect listener. But, as I will try to show, a perfect listener would hear nothing.

The question before us is whether we can suppress rhetoric in favor of communication. A likely instrument for carrying out the suppression is the computer. It turns out, however, that in the process of getting rid of rhetoric, we have gotten rid of communication as well. For we can actually communicate nothing to the machine; we can at best get it to accept the data we feed into it. Nothing can be communicated to a recipient who is not, in principle, free to reject or to ignore the datum he is invited to accept. The issue here is not whether the datum is true or false; it is only whether the recipient can judge it false, or ignore it altogether. Hence, in our dealings with a computer, we have not suppressed rhetoric in favor of communication; we have simply been talking about a situation to which rhetoric and communication are alike irrelevant.

The machine in the version we were just considering failed to serve as an appropriate model of a kind of communication with no rhetorical component because it did not engage in communication at all. It might be thought, however, that by modifying the machine we could create the needed model. If the fault lies in the perfection of perfect communication, let us undo that perfection. Receiving communications imperfectly, the modified machine will, we hope, at least receive them. Rhetoric, however, will still play no part in the message we address to the machine. We can address it rhetorically no more than we can preach to the waves—at least, success in the one enterprise is as unlikely as it is in the other.

Accordingly, let us try to construct a machine to which we cannot communicate perfectly. In fact, we may feel that we do not need to devote much effort to this task. We have merely to shift our perspective on existing machines. When we avowed that we could communicate perfectly to them what we really had in mind were ideal machines, for it is only in theory that a computer would always and of necessity accept, say, the information that N is 15. Now, shifting our perspective slightly, we acknowledge that existing machines are fallible. Mechanical parts wear out; short circuits occur; unexpected "bugs" develop. One cannot at all be sure that an existing machine will accept the information that N is 15.

It does not follow, however, that we are able to communicate with it. For the explanation of its failure is nothing at all like the explanation of human failure. The man fails to accept the datum that N = 15 either because he refuses to believe it or because his mind is not on the printed sheet before him. We could communicate with him if his mind were on what we told him and if he believed it. The machine, however, can neither have its mind on what is being transmitted to it nor receive this datum absent-mindedly; and it can neither believe nor disbelieve what it is told.

Conversely, we may ask whether we would regard ability on the part of the human to accept or reject information in the same way the machine accepts or rejects it as evidence that we could communicate with him. The machine accepts information by passing into a certain state—a certain piece of iron in the machine, for example, is magnetized. Perhaps the closest parallel in the case of a person is posthypnotic suggestion. If the hypnotist succeeds in putting me in a state in which my nose itches whenever I hear the word "freight," he has stimulated me in exactly the way in which a punched card bearing the message "N = 15" stimulates a computer. But no one would say that he had communicated anything to me—indeed, the very point of posthypnotic suggestion is that I be unaware of the suggestion.

We have failed to communicate with the machine because our communication is still perfect. The computer had to accept whatever it did accept. Suppose that instead of accepting the datum that N is 15, the computer stores the value 14 in the location identified with the variable N. This malfunction can undoubtedly be explained, and to explain it is to show why the machine *had* to accept 14 as the value. This value is thus perfectly communicated to it by an errant feature of the situation (for example, by a card reader with a short circuit), even though it is not the value the user intended to communicate to it. The machine's failure, furthermore, is not like the failure of a human to accept a datum. It is not *either* because the machine believes that 15 is not the correct value *or* because its mind is not on what it is doing that it stores 14 as the value. It is only when communication can fail in ways like these that it can occur at all.

It might be supposed that a computer could simulate these human failings. Computers do in fact comment on the programs that are given to them, pointing out syntactical errors and inconsistencies. Why could not a machine be designed to criticize the data fed into it, rejecting those data which, on the basis of one criterion or another, were unacceptable? For example, if N has already been assigned the value of 14, it may be inconsistent to assign it the value 15. The machine I have in mind would say, in effect, (and could say quite explicitly, if we wanted it do) "Hey! Wait a minute! That can't be right!"

When we tell the machine we have just constructed that N is 15, we run a risk. Perhaps it will accept the datum. But it need not. In view of this risk, have we not at last managed to avoid perfect communication with the machine and thus managed to engage in genuine communication with it? If so, we have communication without rhetoric, for, short of magic, we cannot persuade the machine.

There is a difference, however, between the machine's refusal to accept 15 as a datum and a similar refusal on the part of a person. The machine's refusal consists in *telling the user* that 15 is not an acceptable value for N, and in not storing 15 in the appropriate location. The person's refusal, on the other hand, involves *telling himself* that 15 cannot be right. (He may also tell others, though he need not.) The machine does not tell *itself* anything. It is not self-conscious, and hence not conscious of anything. An individual incapable of telling himself, in images if not in words, whatever he is claimed to be conscious of, is not conscious of it. The mere ability to blurt it out is no criterion of consciousness. Now if the computer cannot be said to be conscious that 15 is not an acceptable value of N, even though it tells *us* that it is not acceptable, then it can not be conscious that a datum *is* acceptable when it *is*. But we do not succeed in communicating anything to anyone unless he is conscious of what we are communicating. To say that he must be conscious of what we are communicating is just another way of saying something I said before—that he must be free to accept or reject the datum. The nature of consciousness is the root of the paradox of perfect communication. The communication of a datum could be perfect only if it were in principle impossible for the recipient to tell himself otherwise. But in this case he would be unconscious, and no communication at all would have taken place.[2]

My argument so far has been that we cannot use machines, or systems of them, to illustrate the thesis that there are cases of communication requiring no rhetoric, because machines do not exemplify communication in the first place. As soon as we approach genuine communication, we depart from the world of the machine, and we set foot in a domain requiring rhetoric as an inextricable adjunct or aspect of communication. But this point I have so far made only in a negative way. It cries out for positive argumentation and illustration. Why is rhetoric necessary? What is the indispensable role it plays?

I have just claimed that communication entail consciousness. Without further ado, let me propose a redefinition of rhetoric as the evocation and maintenance of the consciousness required for communication. This new definition is in fact merely a refinement, in the interests of accuracy, of the earlier stipulation that rhetoric "transmits attitudes." Attitudes transmitted from one person to another without passing through the medium of consciousness are the concern of subliminal stimulation, not rhetoric. Rhetoric, furthermore, studies the strategy of altering attitudes *in the service of propositions.* It is concerned not with attitudes as such, but with attitudes adopted *in view of beliefs.* Since it is communication that transmits propositions, rhetoric is thus the adjunct of communication. If art or some other instrumentality alters attitudes apart from their relevance to the acceptance or rejection of propositions, it falls beyond the domain of rhetoric.

The reason rhetoric does not work when applied to the machine is that the latter cannot be conscious of anything. But rhetoric is required whenever there is genuine communication. Let us recall

2. Some readers may wonder why I have gone to such great lengths to show that it is impossible to communicate with machines. To such readers it seems obvious that since machines cannot think, we cannot communicate with them. I do not, however, wish to foreclose the issue whether machines can think. Furthermore, the mathematical theory of communication treats a machine's acceptance of data as a perfectly legitimate example of communication. Not only does such acceptance meet the specifications for communication stipulated by this theory, but it meets them in a certain ideal way—the communication is "noiseless." (See Colin Cherry, *On Human Communication,* Cambridge, Mass., The M.I.T. Press, 1957, especially Ch. 4.) What I am trying to do, in effect, is to introduce a distinction between communication in the mathematical sense and in the sense in which humans participate in it.

the computer user who received the printed statement "N = 15" from the computer. We might be tempted to wonder what role rhetoric could possibly have in this act of straightforward communication. But it was just the fact that the man could have failed to accept the statement that certified his acceptance as the consummation of a genuine act of communication. And rhetoric, whatever else it is, is certainly concerned with the acceptance of or refusal to accept statements. There is a rhetoric of factual communication as well as a rhetoric of exhortation. The facts never speak for themselves; they are always spoken for or against by the rhetorical ambiance of the situation in which they are asserted—an ambiance that is the suppressed premise of the rhetorical enthymeme. Even computer output has rhetorical force, the source of which is in the user himself. If I trust the machine and feel competent to handle it, and am familiar in addition with the general range of values within which the solution of my problem must fall, I endow the machine's output with authority. I can raise questions about the correctness of the output only if I am not completely under the spell of the machine. Most programmers are not; they know that the computer is no more than a device for confronting them with the consequences of their own thinking, exposing its shoddiness to the full light of day when it has been shoddy.

Supposing that all genuine communication does require rhetoric, what does all this have to do with the evocation and maintenance of consciousness? The machine is once again a handy model to serve as the basis of the discussion. Let me begin by mentioning the concept of an *interface*. An interface is the point at which a message passes from one form into another. For example, the card reader, which converts holes in punched cards into electrical impulses, can be regarded as an interface. So can the output printer, and so can a cathode-ray tube into which output might be fed. Now if the phenomenon of "being conscious of" is something that is to occur, or is to have an analogue, in the machine, it seems plausible to look for it in the relation between what lies on one side of an interface and what lies on the other. If there is to be consciousness anywhere in the machine, for example, one might expect to find it in the machine's acceptance, in terms of an electrical response, of the datum on a punched card. For it might seem that the response is the acceptance of a datum quite similar, at least formally, to a person's acceptance of a datum of which he is conscious. But somehow the analogy does not hold; for, as we have seen, there is in fact a radical difference between a person's acceptance of a datum and a machine's acceptance of it. I want to argue that the analogy collapses because, in the sense of "interface" in which interfaces are actually involved in communication, there are really no interfaces at all in the machine; or, alternatively, if we insist on maintaining a sense of "interface" in which there are interfaces in the machine, these latter separate activities that are not separated from each other by any distance of a relevant kind. The relevant kind of distance is that between a person and what is communicated to him. It is this distance that permits him to accept or reject the proffered datum. The reason why such distance is not in fact available to the machine is that it is impossible to maintain the distinction between the two sides of what we take to be the interface. For if the card reader is an interface between punched card and computer, why can we not say, with equal justice, that whatever connects any two elements of the computer is an interface between them? We thus immediately push the concept to triviality. Conversely, we can show that there are in principle no interfaces at all in the system in which the machine is involved, for we can regard the printer as the interface between the output and all of the earlier parts of the train taken together. But if we take these parts together, what is there to prevent us from taking the printer along with them? It seems altogether arbitrary to call the printer an "interface."

Yet even if the concept of an interface cannot be consistently applied to the machine, for the benefit of which it was invented, it can be applied to the reception of messages by people, even though not invented for this purpose. If we elect to say that consciousness is an interface between the computer's output and a person's acceptance or rejection of this output, this statement is not obviously trivial or false in the way that the statement on which it is modeled is. The interface in this case can be neither endlessly proliferated nor eliminated. There is a distance between the person and the datum, but this distance is not to be found everywhere.

We can imagine, furthermore, what it would be like if the interface between the person and the datum were eliminated. One is very often confronted with data of which one is not conscious— the weather report one is not listening to, the striking of the clock; for that matter, any background sound (which is always a datum of *something*). To say that one is not conscious of such data is just to say that there is no distance between oneself and the data—one accepts the data only in a sense in which one could not reject them. Who is to say in this case which is the interface? Is it the vibrating body, the sound waves, the vibrating eardrum, or the cochlea, which converts mechanical into electrical energy? Or is there no interface at all to interrupt the unity of this seamless fabric? Whichever way we look at the activity in question, it is one in which the person is sometimes engaged and in which the machine is always engaged.

It now becomes evident what would be required if we were to succeed in communicating with the machine. We would have to introduce a genuine interface between the machine and the datum we wished to communicate to it. Is it not clear, however, that in the entire world of physical things, of which the machine is a part, there is no genuine interface? Nothing is sufficiently *other* than the machine to be communicated to it. Only what is other than a person can be communicated to him.

To be conscious of something is always to interrupt the unity of the transaction between subject and object. Consciousness confronts the person with something radically other than himself. I have the power to accept or reject a datum only because I am not the datum. The question that now seems most imperative to deal with is "How can two beings that are radically different be brought into relation to each other at all?" I have already argued in the last chapter that no consistent answer to this question is possible. Consciousness is a contradiction which consists in bringing together the poles of contradiction. But without consciousness, there could be no distinction between the person and a datum other than that person; no interface could ultimately be maintained. For that matter, without the distinction between person and datum there could be no consciousness. If consciousness is a contradiction, let us not presume that it accordingly does not exist; it is only in a world in which all problems have been swept under the rug that there are no contradictions.

An interface is a kind of wedge as well as a kind of bridge, and rhetoric is the technique of driving this wedge between a person and the data of his immediate experience. We have seen how rhetoric of factual communication can drive it. Just as the data of sensuous experience can constitute a background from which the person is not separated, so can data in a more technical sense. The computer operator sits idly by while the machine spews forth page after page of numbers arranged in columns. To him, this flow of printed paper is just an aspect of the metabolism of a healthy machine. He takes it in, just as the machine itself has taken in the data on the punched cards fed to it. The user to whom the printed sheets are eventually handed may also merely take in the numbers. He may simply accept them as the machine accepts data. But he need not. A distance may be interposed between him and the numbers. The force that interposes it is the rhetoric of objective communication and the source of this rhetoric, as we have already seen, is in the user himself. He has an idea what the numbers ought to be like, and if they fail to conform to his idea, he suddenly begins to view them with suspicion. If he does, his consciousness of the numbers has been evoked by his own previous state; he has moved himself. Objective data are communicated, of course, by other persons as well as by machines. In both cases, the source of the rhetoric required to evoke consciousness in the recipient can lie wholly within the recipient himself. The fact that the person who communicates the data need not engage in rhetoric in the act of communicating them has made it appear that no rhetoric at all is involved in objective communication. If it were not, however, communication would collapse into mere acceptance of data *à la* machine.

A reflexive rhetoric of objective communication has not generally been recognized. It is perhaps more plausible, however, to characterize the irreflexive rhetoric that applies to the other domains of discourse in the same terms as those in which we have characterized the reflexive rhetoric. It, too, seeks to evoke and maintain consciousness—in this case, consciousness on the part of someone other than the user of the rhetoric. What is attacked by both the irreflexive rhetoric of belief and the irreflexive rhetoric of action is just unconsciousness in all its forms: unawareness, naive acceptance, shortsightedness, complacency, blind confidence, unquestioning conformity to habits of thought and action, or the taking for granted of the personal qualities of a distinguished man. The senses have long been held to dull the mind, and the rhetoric of the Puritan is once again intended to evoke a heightened consciousness. Of course consciousness is a matter of relativity; he who is conscious of some things will perforce be unconscious of others. This is precisely why the use of rhetoric generates controversy. If I take the position that you are unconscious of the need for upholding the law in a democracy, you may find me unconscious of the moral issues that have made you decide to take the law into your own hands.

This book is not the place to carry out an exhaustive comparison between my conception of the nature of rhetoric and all the others that have been widely adopted. But it is surely incumbent upon me to compare my conception with the conception of rhetoric as the art of persuasion, since this had been by far the most widely held. One of the shoals on which this conception continually threatens to founder is the distinction between persuasion that is the legitimate concern of rhetoric, and persuasion that is not. Where shall we draw the line between subliminal stimulation, coercion at gunpoint, and brainwashing, on the one hand, and rhetorical persuasion on the other? I would argue that it is natural to draw the line in terms of the evocation of consciousness for purposes of communication. Subliminal stimulation deliberately avoids consciousness. It attempts to dissolve the interface between person and datum. The armed bandit evokes fear, not consciousness. Brainwashing depends on a physiological deprivation. Although we may say that it *causes* a state of consciousness, it would be incorrect to hold that it *evokes* the state. Unless we are taking poetic liberties we do not say that *A* evokes *B* when *A* merely causes *B*. The wind does not evoke the slamming of the door.

If rhetoric is no more than the art of persuasion, we will have a difficult time convincing the rationalists and positivists that it is really necessary. We have indeed had this difficulty throughout the centuries. When men see the truth, say the rationalists and positivists, they do not need to be persuaded of anything. Persuasion holds sway only in that twilight zone in which there is neither formal truth nor objective fact. But that zone will some day be abolished.

I think I have indicated how I would reply to the rationalist and the positivist. Rhetoric, in my view, permeates even formal truth and objective fact. Even in the utopian world envisaged by my interlocutors, people must still manage to remain conscious for if they do not, communication will become perfect and collapse into noncommunication, and there will no longer be a world at all—only a system comparable to a machine or system of machines.

My discussion of computers and of rhetoric may seem to have taken me far afield from the problem of other minds. But an insight into the problem is in fact close at hand. This insight arises, oddly enough, from the possibility of a reflexive rhetoric of objective fact. The reason it seems odd that this possibility should be a source of help with the problem of other minds is that it can perfectly characterize a solitary thinker. When a person scanning computer output is suddenly brought to see something he had not seen before, and to express incredulity, where are the other minds?

In order to answer this question, let us note that "the problem of other minds," if it arises at all, arises with respect to my own mind as well as to that of another. Consider, for example, my account of the person I was last year. It is surely at least as open to doubt as the account I render of your state of mind at this moment. Autobiography is not notably more reliable than biography. And of course, precisely the same unreliability that infects my account of myself as of a year ago would also infect my account of myself as of a second ago. I cannot hope to recapture either my remote or my immediate youth. But of course, youth is only a way of looking at things—a point of view. It is the point of view that defined me in my full actuality a year or a second ago.

The man perusing the output is subject to a reflexive rhetoric precisely because his mind of this moment is not his mind of two weeks ago, when he began to write the program that eventually produced the printout he has in his hands. It is that earlier mind which is addressing him now, telling him that he ought to accept the output or be suspicious of it. It is that earlier mind which goads him into consciousness; if he had no access to that earlier mind, he could not now be conscious, but could only be accepting data as the machine accepts data. Hence, from the possibility of distinguishing a machine's acceptance of data from a person's, it follows that a person has access to his past minds.

This development may not seem to have helped much. We are still confronted by the need to show that minds other than past minds of one person exist. *Prima facie* evidence for this conclusion is that we normally think of rhetoric as nonreflexive. Usually, it is another person who evokes consciousness in a given individual. Reflexive rhetoric is a very special case of this transaction—so special, indeed, that it has received little mention in the history of rhetoric.[3]

Such a *prima facie* consideration, however, may not strike the reader as an at all satisfying way of bridging the gap between one person's mind and the minds of others. My example has concerned the relation between a solitary person and a machine. On what

3. But see Perelman and Olbrechts–Tyteca, *La Nouvelle Rhétorique: Traité de l'Argumentation*, Paris, Presses Universitaires de France, 1958, §9.

grounds, it may be asked, can I be sure that what I take to be other people are not in fact machines, the output from which I interpret in the light of past states of my own mind?

Perhaps they are; I cannot guarantee that machines will never totally surround and isolate me. But such a state of affairs is contingent, not necessary. As long as I can react to past minds of my own, there is no reason why *in principle* I cannot react to the present minds of other persons, supposing that there are other persons nearby. If other persons are nearby, I can tell that they are persons in ways that do not beg the question of whether they are conscious or have states of mind. For example, I can be aware of another as the source of a rhetoric not my own. Hence I am not *in principle* cut off from others, as I am on the view of the skeptic who defends the thesis of privileged access.

The old analogical argument to "other minds" crosses the gulf between my mind and others by asserting that because I see that the others are persons, I infer that they have minds like my own. For me, however, the gulf is already crossed before we get to the other persons. I cross it in being subject to the rhetoric of my own "other minds." The move to other persons, then, is but a matter of detail.

It may be objected, however, that I have localized the problem in a domain to which privileged access is irrelevant, and thus that I have failed to come to grips with it. The problem, it might be said, does not arise *apropos* a person's knowledge of past states of his own mind. It arises rather in terms of the *contrast* between his knowledge of the past states of his own mind and his knowledge of corresponding states of the minds of others. Thus even though I may describe a past state in terms that no longer seem altogether trustworthy to me ("I was under the influence of Existentialism when I wrote that" —but this statement may simply be untrue, even though it is the best I can produce now), there are ways in which I have access to past states that others do not have. I *remember* that splitting headache I had yesterday. If *you* remember it, however, all that you remember is my behavior; you cannot remember my headache as I do. The skeptical gap seems to have opened up between my knowledge of a past mind and your memory of that same mind.

The answer is that memory is a form of consciousness. If I remember the headache, some rhetoric is at work, something that drives a wedge between the datum and myself. The distance opened up by this wedge is no less intergalactic than any distance that could intervene between another person and myself. Not even the head-ache of the present moment can be snatched back from the brink of this abyss. I am conscious of my headache only because my attention has been called to it. If I were less alert, or if my attention were riveted to a life-and-death emergency, I would not be conscious of it. The very absence of such an emergency is a factor in the reflexive rhetoric through which I become aware of my own headache. There is also a rhetoric that calls *your* headache to my attention—a rhetoric much practised in TV commercials. To be sure, it is different from the reflexive rhetoric that calls *my* headache to my attention, but it is not radically less reliable.

A critic might concede the points I have just made, precisely in order to attack me. "You have now abolished the problem of other minds," he might say. "But wasn't it your criticism of the solipsist that *he* abolishes the problem? You stated that the self emerges pre-cisely because there is a problem. But now you say there is no prob-lem. How, then, is your argument relevant in your own terms to a discussion of the self?"

My reply is that I have not abolished the problem that gives rise to the self when we reflect upon the existence and contents of other minds. This is the problem posed by the insertion of the rhetorical wedge: How can one be *conscious* of something from which he is *separated*? Or, as I put the question earlier in this chaper, "How can two beings that are radically different be brought into rela-tion at all?" The problem, in other words, is just the problem of consciousness itself. The question "How can I be conscious of the contents of other minds?" is part of a more general question.

It remains to be shown, however, why it has been supposed that there was a special problem concerned with other minds. In carry-ing out the explanation it is useful to refer again to the rhetoric through which we become aware of another person's mental states. That rhetoric can be so powerful that it induces the same states in us. A person in the grip of violent emotions can fill us with the same emotions. One who witnesses severe beating can himself suffer the pain of the beating. Empathy of this sort is common; when it occurs it threatens the empathizer with engulfment, for his mind is swamped by the contents of the other's mind. If he regards himself as a unique being, however, he may resist this engulfment. He may draw a line between his own mental contents and those of others. With a single stroke, he assumes both his own privacy and the inaccessibility of the other. In systematically denying others access to his consciousness, he is systematically denying himself access to the consciousness of others. Thus the negation that systematically excludes the other is needed to establish him as unique.

It might be objected that this dialectic is questionable. Why, after all, can I not impute privacy to myself without imputing inaccessibility to others? The answer is that if the consciousness of the other were completely accessible to me, there would be no point in claiming privacy for myself. The uniqueness I claim is uniqueness in a world of persons. Creatures that I know through and through are not persons, and in a world of such creatures the question of my uniqueness could not arise. There is an analogy to this in the dialectic of physical privacy. Even a modest person has no hesitation in disrobing in front of animals unless he regards them as to some extent living a life inaccessible to him—a life in which there can be secret knowledge. Hence my physical privacy is never an issue for me unless the physical privacy of those around me could be an issue for them. This dialectic is presupposed by the Sartrean *look,* since only the look of an eye assumed to be human can evoke shame in the one who is conscious of being looked at. But Sartre does not say how we could ever come to make the assumption that a human eye is looking at us. On my view, it is my privacy that requires the inaccessibility of others. In the passage quoted as the motto of this Chapter, Husserl seems to assume that this dialectic is primordial. Surely, however, there are cultures and individuals which have not engaged in it, for which neither privacy nor inaccessibility would be important ideas.

The reader may at this point be reminded of certain asymmetries I have endorsed, particularly in Chapters 4 and 6. I asserted that no one can share with another his conception of himself as a totality, and that a person may impute irreplaceability to himself. These assertions may suggest a position on other minds inconsistent with the one I have just been expounding, according to which mental contents are shareable at least when an act of violence forces us temporarily to abandon the dialectic of privacy. This inconsistency, however, can readily be resolved; the distinction needed is between contents of which we can be conscious and structures of which we cannot. Although I can be conscious of my own past headache, or even, with appropriate rhetoric, of your present one, I cannot be said to be conscious of my conception of myself as a totality. Perhaps I can be conscious of aspects of this conception, but I cannot be conscious of all of it at once. It is a regulative idea, as is the irreplaceability within my own world that I impute to myself. I cannot express or even formulate the place I think I occupy in this world.

To summarize the conclusions of this rather obliquely argued chapter, I began by pointing out that communication presupposes other minds. Genuine communication, as distinct from the act of feeding data to a machine, is characterized by a rhetorical component. Rhetoric is present even when a solitary person is receiving information from the machine (or from some other impersonal source); it is a reflexive rhetoric addressed to the present mind of the person by some past mind. If this reflexive rhetoric is possible, so is rhetoric in general; if what I was in the past can address what I am now, there is no reason in principle why I cannot address you and, having caught your attention, tell you anything I want you to know. Hence it is the possibility of distinguishing genuine communication from machine input that established the accessibility of other minds. This accessibility is a special case of the availability of any object to consciousness. It requires an interface to be driven between consciousness and its object. This interface separates consciousness from its object, providing the distance that is at the heart of the paradox of consciousness. That there is a paradox in our having access to other minds is just a special case of the paradox of consciousness in general.

10 · CONTROVERSY AND THE SELF

*A principle which everyone must accept who understands anything
that is, is not a hypothesis.*—Aristotle

So far in this book I have considered the relations between the
concept of the self and a variety of other concepts, including
freedom, uniqueness, death, consciousness, and other minds. My
treatment of such concepts might be said to be transcultural,
because my discussion has not been bound to particular civiliza-
tions or historical periods. In talking about freedom, for example,
I have not adduced any considerations peculiar to any one culture
in which the concept of freedom has arisen. To put the matter
pejoratively, my discussion has been narrowly epistemological or
metaphysical. Yet it has sometimes been claimed that the self is
bound to culture, at least as the locus of acculturation. According
to this claim, the difference between the contemporary German and
the ancient Greek is an irreducible qualitative difference in selves.
The self reflects its polar opposite, the world of culture, and when
such worlds are incommensurable, so are the selves that reflect them.

In times of rapid cultural change such as our own, it is not
easy to think of the self as simply the locus of acculturation. In
one lifetime, a person can be subject to the pull of a succession
of cultures, and the question arises how this pull is possible.
Unless some component of the self transcends acculturation, how
can a self defined through one world respond to the solicitation
of another world? This is the question to which I shall address
myself in this chapter. Although the question concerns cultures,
I find it convenient to answer it in terms of philosophical systems.
It is easier to be precise in setting forth the content of a philosophical system than in setting forth the content of a culture.
Clearly, however, if we think of cultures as incommensurable, what

we have in mind is precisely the respect in which they function as philosophical systems.

It has often been held that between two rival philosophical systems there is at least sometimes a gulf which neither position can cross if it insists on pursuing the discussion in its own terms.[1] "Each . . . can claim the virtues of the other . . . while denying that the other . . . in fact possesses those virtues," as McKeon says.[2] I have myself expressed this view by asserting that the partisan of each system is, in principle, incapable of conceiving the system espoused by the other. "For each, in stating his own systematic position, is in effect claiming that this position includes all the relevant evidence and therefore no statement adducing evidence against it is possible."[3] To some readers, this assertion sounds strange. Surely, they will object, one can *conceive* of a rival system, even though one violently disagrees with it. Indeed, how could one disagree with it at all unless one could conceive of it? This is a problem to which I wish to address myself in this chapter. However, I see no reason to withdraw my assertion that a philosopher who espouses one system is incapable of conceiving of a rival system. If it were merely the case that he had reviewed the evidence for the rival system, and found it unconvincing, I would certainly admit that he could conceive of the rival system. But when a philosopher—say Smith—is in principle committed to the thesis that nothing that his antagonist submits as evidence can possibly be evidence for anything except Smith's own view, then to say that Smith literally cannot conceive of his antagonist's system seems to me an accurate way of describing the situation. Another way of putting the matter is to point out that philosophical positions are not hypotheses. If one frames a hypothesis, one can regard a rival hypothesis as a possibility. But one does not take a philosophical position as the result of choosing among positions regarded as possible. The position one takes is really the only one that one sees as possible; and one sees one's rival's positions, accordingly, as impossible. But one cannot conceive the impossible. One can no

---

1. See, for example, Eberhard Rogge, *Axiomatik alles möglichen Philosophierens,* Meisenheim/Glan: Westkulturverlag Anton Hain, 1950; Richard McKeon, "Philosophy and Method," *The Journal of Philosophy,* Vol. 48, 1951, pp. 653–682; and Everett Hall, *Philosophical Systems, A Categorial Analysis,* Chicago, University of Chicago Press, 1960.
2. *Op. cit.,* p. 673.
3. *Philosophy and Argument,* University Park: The Pennsylvania State University Press, 1959, p. 1.

doubt talk, and perhaps in a sense even think, about round squares even if one cannot conceive of them, but no one is in fact able to form the idea of a round square. Similarly, no philosopher taking a systematic position is in principle able to form the idea of a position contradicting his. A statement expressing a philosophical system is like a tautology in logic. Any tautology includes all the possible evidence; it is true regardless of the evidence. Hence no evidence against a tautology is possible. And if we contradict a tautology, the result is a contradiction; that is, a statement the meaning of which we literally cannot conceive. The difference between tautologies and philosophical systems, however, is that while all rational beings admit the same set of tautologies, not all rational beings endorse the same philosophical system.

In an interesting article,[4] Duane Whittier has reviewed a number of situations in which the advocate of a philosophical system cannot envisage the possibility of evidence contradicting it. One of these is the dispute over the "incommunicability of content":

> It has been asserted that there is no way of knowing for certain that when two persons name color-sensations alike they are actually experiencing the same sensation-quality. It is said that it is *conceivable* that color-sensations between persons might differ systematically in such a way as to elude any test for the difference. Critics of this view argue that this state-of-affairs is not conceivable because what we *mean* by the expressions "the same" and "different experience" is determined, and can only be determined, by public criteria. To speak of a color-blindness that no test can detect is to speak idly. What we *mean* by "color-blindness" or "sensation-discrepancy" is precisely those things which certain tests reveal. For one party to this dispute such color-experience discrepancy is *conceivable*. To a verificationist theory of meaning it is not conceivable.[5]

From the point of view of the philosopher who interprets color-blindness as a phenomenon exhaustively defined in terms of public criteria—the verificationist—it is logically impossible that there should be any cases of color-blindness not satisfying these criteria. His interpretation of color-blindness renders him incapable of conceiving such cases, just as the standard definition of a circle renders us incapable of conceiving a square circle. It might be

---

4. "Basic Assumption and Argument in Philosophy," *The Monist,* Vol. 48, 1964, pp. 486–500.
5. *Ibid.,* p. 488.

objected that this analogy is defective, since although we *cannot* interpret circles in such a way as to be able to conceive a square circle, we *can* interpret color-blindness in such a way as to be able to conceive cases of color-blindness not satisfying the public criteria. But the verificationist, unlike other people, *cannot* in fact conceive any cases of color-blindness not satisfying the public criteria, for it is his very commitment to his position that cuts him off from this possibility. This is precisely to say that he cannot conceive of any evidence against the view that all cases of color-blindness satisfy the public criteria. Whatever he will accept as evidence must already satisfy the public criteria. Hence all the evidence that is possible is evidence for his own view. He is in much the same position as that of a person who, on being told that circles can be square, asks for evidence of this possibility. All that he, or anyone else, is willing to regard as evidence at all must take the form of circles that are not square.

But there is an important difference between asserting that no circles are square and asserting that no cases of color-blindness fail to satisfy the public criteria. The latter assertion is polemical. It is made in order to challenge the contention that there might be cases of color-blindness not satisfying the public criteria; the former assertion, on the other hand, is not made in order to challenge the contention that circles can be square. That is not a serious contention at all. The reason why we assert "No circles are square" is rather that we deduce it from a definition of "circle," the function of which is regulative rather than polemical. Such a definition is not the formulation of a view about circles. It expresses the nature of a circle, but this expression is not a view. There are alternatives to any view, just because it is a view and not the grasp of a fact. However, all correct expressions of the nature of a circle (at least in Euclidean space) are equivalent, because they all express the same fact. Because the definition of "circle" is not a view, it cannot be used to *attack* a view about circles.

In fact, if anyone contends that circles can be square, he is neither expressing nor attacking a view about circles. He is not saying "I interpret circles in this new way." All that he is doing, in effect, is proposing that the term "circle" be broadened to include squares. We can argue with him over the usefulness of this proposal, but our argument will not be an attempt of any sort to get our hearers to interpret circles in one way rather than another.[6] There is only one way to interpret circles—hence we do not interpret them at all.

The assertion "No cases of color-blindness fail to satisfy the public criteria," however, arises in the effort to combat a certain interpretation of color-blindness, and thus is itself an interpretation. It interprets color-blindness as nothing more than a certain sequence of responses to certain tests capable of being conducted in public. This is not only an interpretation of color-blindness, it is a very narrow and tendentious interpretation; many people would call it altogether perverse. It certainly does not answer to what most people mean by "color-blindness." The only excuse for making such an assertion as this is that in making it one intends to attack another interpretation that seems to have consequences at least equally perverse. In this case the unwelcome consequence is the possibility of undetectable cases of color-blindness.

I have said that for the verificationist there can be no evidence contradicting his view. He literally cannot conceive of any case of color-blindness not satisfying the public criteria. If anyone contends that such cases are possible the verificationist may, of course, imagine that his interlocutor is proposing that the term "color-blindness" be broadened. But as in the case of the proposal that the term "circle" be broadened, such a proposal is not seen as an interpretation of color-blindness, and hence is not regarded by the verificationist as an interpretation at variance with his own. As a purely verbal proposal, it does not, so far as he can see, express a genuine alternative to his view.[7]

But if a philosopher literally cannot conceive of any genuine alternative to his view, then he cannot understand his own position as a view that has arisen as a response to an alternative view. Asked why he takes the position he does, he is not entitled to say "There is a perverse view that I wish to attack." All that he can say is "I am simply stating the nature of color-blindness." But to an onlooker, this explanation is obviously wrong. No one who was

6. So committed are the verificationists to their view that they are unable to see it, or any other view, as a view. To them all philosophical contentions are nothing but proposals to use terms in certain ways—proposals which can be evaluated only in terms of their "usefulness." See, for example, Carnap, *The Logical Syntax of Language*, London, Kegan Paul, Trench, Trubner & Co., 1937, pp. 277–81, 301. But the verificationists consistently refuse to say what they mean by "usefulness" in this connection.
7. Thus for Carnap; see footnote 6.

simply stating the nature of color-blindness would define it in terms of the satisfaction of public criteria. Any who defined it in such a perverse way could have done so only in order to attack an alien view. A definition as strange as this does not arise in a vacuum.

In fact, the verificationist is aware of the context of his own definition. Even though his position does not *entitle* him to conceive of any genuine alternative, yet he will cheerfully admit that it arises from a concern with an alternative, and will sincerely impugn this alternative as perverse. The notion of developing his definition in total isolation from the alleged error that it aims to correct will seem just as queer to him as it does to others.

The verificationist has contradicted himself. He has said, in effect, both "my position is not a view" and "my position is a view, which attacks a rival view."[8] He both can conceive of an alternative to his position and cannot conceive of an alternative to it.

Let us analyze the contradiction in greater detail. It arises from two considerations. In the first place, as I have already said, a philosopher does not take his position as the result of choosing among positions he regards as possible. The position he takes is actually the only one that he sees as possible. It follows that he must regard all rival positions as impossible. "Impossible" here means "logically impossible"; it is not merely a psychological block or a defect in imagination that prevents the philosopher from conceiving a rival position. His inability to conceive it is instead like anyone's inability to conceive a logical contradiction.

The second consideration is that the philosopher's position is polemically oriented; it does not arise in a vacuum. It is a view that arises in the attempt to combat an alien view. But no one would think of attempting to combat a view that he did not regard as logically possible. If someone tells me that some squares are not squares, I simply do not know what he means. If I do not know what he means, I am not in a position to regard his statement as the expression of a perverse or dangerous doctrine that I want to attack. I can want to attack a doctrine only if I see it as logically possible.

Another way to put this second consideration is in terms suggested earlier. If I cannot conceive any alternative to my view,

8. Notice that I use the term "position" here to include both definitions that are not interpretations—for example, the definition of "circle"—and views, such as the verificationist's.

then my view, like a logical tautology, conveys no information; it is true for all possible worlds. But again like a tautology, it is trivially true. If my view is to be true in a nontrivial way, then at least one alternative to it must be conceivable.

Hence the verificationist must see the view he is attacking as both logically impossible and logically possible. This is a contradiction. One's normal reaction to a contradiction is to look for a distinction in terms of which it can be resolved. But it is clear that in the present case no saving distinction can be found. It is in precisely the same sense of "logically possible" that the alternative to the philosopher's position must be both logically *possible* and logically *im*possible. In fact, it is because the alternative is logically possible that it is logically impossible, and it is because it is logically impossible that it is logically possible. A view can be negated (that is, called logically impossible) only if it exists (that is, is logically possible) and it can exist only if it can be negated (for otherwise it is just a tautology or other analytically true statement, not a view). Furthermore, any philosophical view arises precisely as the negation of another view.

If there were a way of resolving the contradiction, the dialectical tension between the position that all cases of color-blindness must satisfy public criteria and the alternative to this position would be broken, and both the position and the alternative would collapse into inanity. Either the philosopher would find himself entertaining the alternative to his position as one possibility among many, or he would find that the point of taking his position had vanished.

It would be preposterous to argue that verificationists, or philosophers who take any other view, are explicitly aware of embracing a contradiction. Most philosophers would be horrified by the very suggestion. Throughout the history of philosophy, only a handful of thinkers have made the accusation that I am making. In a somewhat different version, however, the accusation is slightly more palatable. This version is a consequence of some reflections on argumentative strategies open to the philosopher. I have pointed out that if a philosopher defines color-blindness in terms of the satisfaction of public criteria, he will be unable to accept as evidence any alleged evidence of the existence of color-blindness failing to satisfy the public criteria. He can thus argue by pointing to all the evidence amassed in favor of his view, and by disqualifying any alleged evidence against it. But an astute opponent will soon see that in carrying out each of these strategies the philosopher is doing no more than begging the question. If the proposition to be proved is that all the evidence is in his favor, the proof cannot consist in any application of that proposition itself. Hence the verificationist philosopher may turn to a new strategy. This consists in exposing an incoherence internal to the view that some cases of color-blindness do not satisfy public criteria. One might argue as follows: If there can be cases of color-blindness not satisfying public criteria, then there is no reason in principle why there should not be cases of insensateness of other sorts not satisfying public criteria; for example, tone-deafness or a corresponding olfactory defect. There is no reason, for that matter, why it should simply be *defects* in sensation that might be undetectable, for the same principle that leads us to suspect that undetectable defects are possible should also lead us to suspect that undetectable differences in *qualia* are possible. Perhaps what you call red is what I call green. The fact that there are public criteria to enable us to determine whether a person sees red is irrelevant; even when you behave in such a way that according to these criteria you are seeing red, you may still be seeing what I call green. This brings us to final and fatal extension of the position, which has been well expressed by Max Black:

> The very same considerations which inculcate scepticism concerning the individual *qualia* of another person's experiences ought to raise insuperable doubts concerning the character of the classes to which they belong. If we cannot be sure that another person means by "red" or "middle C" the same as ourselves, we have no better ground for believing that such relatively general terms as "sensations," "sense-quality," or "feeling" mean the same to hearer and speaker. We cannot even be sure that the names of colors and tastes apply at all to sensory experience rather than to some features of, say, logical deduction.[9]

But exactly the same considerations apply to the *entire vocabulary* of the man who has said that there may be undetectable cases of color-blindness. Given any word that he uses, there is no way of being sure that he means by the word what we do. On his own view, then, "we ought to be in no position to understand *any* of his own

9. *Language and Philosophy*, Ithaca, New York, Cornell University Press, 1949, p. 6.

statements. . . . Only [he] can ever know what he means by his sceptical assertions; and he can never tell us."[10]

Black summarizes by saying of the view under attack that it "involves a very peculiar type of *reductio ad absurdum*. For if [the] thesis were true, it would be *meaningless* to us; therefore we cannot be expected to understand it; therefore we cannot be expected to believe it."[11] The argument that exposes this *reductio* might also be said to be of a peculiar type. It is peculiar in that it is an *argumentum ad hominem*, an argument of a type that is not usually regarded as rigorous. But the reason why *argumentum ad hominem* is not usually regarded as rigorous is that stronger arguments are usually available which appeal to evidence; they are *ad rem* rather than *ad hominem*. Where every appeal to evidence is question-begging, however, as it would be in the case of the verificationist, there can be no stronger argument than *argumentum ad hominem*.[12]

Yet there is an *argumentum ad hominem* against this very use of *argumentum ad hominem*. I have just said that the validity of this use arises from the invalidity of any appeal to evidence. The appeal to evidence is invalid because by hypothesis no evidence in favor of the view that there may be undetectable cases of color-blindness is possible. This is tantamount to saying that this view is inconceivable. The *argumentum ad hominem*, however, is precisely an exercise in conceiving the view under attack. It is essentially a sympathetic argument—one that slays by delivering "the kiss of death." To destroy a view, its opponent simply assumes its leading principle and elicits the fatal consequences of that principle. But one cannot assume a principle if one cannot conceive it. Thus a dilemma arises: either the verificationist can conceive the view he attacks, or not. If he can conceive it, *argumentum ad hominem* is no longer an effective argument; a far more relevant attack will be one that appeals to evidence. But if he cannot conceive the view he wishes to attack, he cannot formulate an *argumentum ad hominem*. That this dilemma is itself addressed *ad hominem* is shown by the way in which it exploits the assumption that any *argumentum ad hominem* must exploit an assump-

10. *Ibid.*, p. 7.
11. *Ibid.*
12. I have defended this contention in "Philosophy and *Argumentum ad Hominem*," *The Journal of Philosophy*, Vol. 49, No. 15, 1952, pp. 489–98. See also *Philosophy and Argument*, Ch. VI.

tion. The dilemma exploits this assumption by pointing out that one cannot exploit any assumption without first conceiving it.

Hence the verificationist is caught once again in a contradiction. He must both be unable to conceive the view he attacks and be able to conceive it. There is no way in which he can avoid this contradiction.

Exactly the same considerations that apply to the particular philosophical views on which I have chosen to dwell thus far in this chapter would apply to any philosophical view whatever. Whoever adopts a philosophy adopts a contradiction, whether he knows it or not. This fact is seen most clearly when we consider the argumentative strategies open to a philosopher, as we have just done.

Either of two different responses to this situation would be entirely natural. One is to give up philosophy. The difficulties inherent in this response are well known. Anyone who deliberately sets out to give up philosophy takes a view that can only be regarded as itself philosophical. The other response is to abandon the attempt to avoid contradiction. But this irrationalism undercuts itself too. For it is only as a consequence of attempting to avoid contradiction that we fall into it. If the rational expression of our views were never a desideratum, the very concept of contradiction could not arise. There are no contradictions in nature; whatever natural thing we choose, it cannot both have a certain property and not have it; in nature, the Law of Noncontradiction reigns supreme. There are no contradictions in the utterances of animals or idiots— one grunt does not contradict another, and a parrot is not held accountable for its speech, however inconsistent. Contradictions exist only in the language of men attempting to be consistent. To waive the goal of consistency is thus to abolish the very possibility of contradiction.

The response that I want to recommend—the only response, I think, that does not undermine itself—is to accept the fact that in espousing a philosophical view one has contradicted oneself, while at the same time maintaining consistency as the standard and goal of discourse. The philosopher who regretfully accepts the fact that in taking a view and opposing other views he has contradicted himself differs markedly from the one who does not accept this fact. The latter is a kind of schizophrene. Sometimes he regards a view that he opposes as logically possible. Sometimes he regards the same view as logically impossible. He thinks of it as logically possible when he wants to attack it. His attack, however, consists in exhibiting it as logically impossible. He vacillates between these two assessments of the view he opposes. He adopts one after the other, failing to see that in fact both assessments apply to the same view at the same time and in the same respect. By introducing a specious temporal interval between the assessments, he has managed momentarily to evade the contradiction by keeping its poles apart, but the evasion is not a genuine escape; it is only a dissimulation. To stop dissimulating, one must accept the contradiction; one must acknowledge that both assessments coincide. One must be willing to unify the poles. Indeed, the contradiction itself presupposes this unification. Unless there is a single perspective from which an opposing view can be seen as both logically possible and logically impossible, there is no contradiction—there is only a vacillation. It might be objected that the contradiction exists regardless of perspective. Unsuspected contradictions, after all, have been known to lurk in mathematical systems. But I have already pointed out that contradictions exist only for people attempting to avoid them. Men concerned with mathematical systems are obviously attempting to avoid contradictions. It is this very attempt, however, that results in the single perspective from which it is possible to assert that p and not-p are both true at the same time and in the same respect. It is because the vacillator is not interested in avoiding contradictions, on the other hand, that there are no contradictions for him to avoid.

Let us examine more closely the perspective from which the poles of a contradiction are unified. This perspective is a locus of responsibility. For it is clear that only the thinker who refuses to vacillate between the poles is a responsible thinker—he has assumed responsibility for his own philosophical view. Indeed, the mode of existence of a responsibility closely resembles the mode of existence of a contradiction. Just as contradictions exist only for those attempting to avoid them, so responsibilities exist only for those willing to assume them. Neither contradictions nor responsibilities exist in nature. In Chapter 5, I have already discussed the relation between contradictions and responsibilities.

The perspective from which the poles of a contradiction are unified is also a locus of transcendence, for the philosopher who sees an opposing view as both logically impossible and logically possible stands both inside his own view and outside it. The assessment of the opposing view as logically impossible is one that the philosopher must make from within his own view, since it is the way in which his view defines its terms that renders any alternative view inconceivable to him. The assessment of the opposing view as logically possible, on the other hand, presupposes that the philosopher stands outside his own view, observing how the latter is saved from triviality by the existence of meaningful assertions inconsistent with it. The kind of transcendence that is involved in the philosopher's acceptance of the two contradictory assessments of a rival view is an example of what I have been calling ecstasis. It is a characteristic of "a being which in its being is what it is not, and is not what it is." The responsible philosophical thinker is both totally immersed in his point of view and not totally immersed in it—and thus his being as a responsible thinker consists in his being what he is not and not being what he is.

In addition, the perspective is a locus of subjectivity. As I have said several times, contradictions do not occur in nature. They do not occur in any objective domain. Indeed, a domain has objectivity to the extent that the Law of Noncontradiction is valid within it; even a fantasy world is objective to the extent that within that world nothing both has a certain property and fails to have it at the same time in the same respect. It follows that the sole domain of contradictions must be subjectivity. When we accept a contradiction we accordingly acknowledge the subjectivity of our perspective. This is a point I made in Chapter 8.

The conclusion I wish to draw is obvious. It is the *self* to which responsibility, transcendence, and subjectivity have traditionally been ascribed. The *self,* then, is the perspective from which the poles of a contradiction are unified. The contradiction presupposes the self. At the same time, it takes a contradiction to evoke the self. The contradiction is a burden which the self arises to take up. There is no other occasion on which the self is called for.

The self is the pivot of philosophical controversy. One can address arguments only to the thinker willing to acknowledge a contradiction when one occurs, and yet committed to the principle that discourse should be consistent. It would be impossible, for example, to argue with the schizophrene who sometimes sees his opponent's view as logically possible and sometimes sees it as logically impossible, but sees no contradiction. I do not mean to suggest, however, that it is only the philosopher under attack in whom the self must have arisen. It must also have arisen in the attacker. Otherwise, the attack will be no more than an exercise in logic-chopping. An attacker who insists that those whom he attacks take seriously the contradictions into which they have fallen, but who refuses to apply the same standard to himself can be safely ignored, for he is in fact a schizophrene. Unless a man is willing to reveal the stake he has in criticizing another position, we need not listen to his criticism. I have already suggested the nature of that stake. All effective philosophical arguments are *ad hominem,* but there is an *argumentum ad hominem* against the use of any *argumentum ad hominem*—a meta-*argumentum ad hominem* that consists in pointing out that in order to use *argumentum ad hominem* one must stand both inside one's own view and outside it. The price the philosophical critic must pay for his use of *argumentum ad hominem* is to be subject to this meta-*argumentum ad hominem.* If he refuses to pay this price his talk becomes mere schizophrenic babble. It takes a self to evoke a self.

The act in which the self is evoked is essentially an act of philosophical criticism because it is only in responding to such criticism that we are forced to stand outside ourselves. The proper response to nonphilosophical criticism is not ecstasis but the correction of our errors. Hence not only is the self the pivot of philosophical controversy, but also philosophical controversy is the life-sustaining atmosphere of the self.

By "philosophical controversy" I do not, of course mean only debate among academic philosophers over issues traditionally identified as philosophical. The preceding chapters can be taken as an attempt to exhibit the philosophical character of the tensions that generate the self-tensions such as those involved in the contemplation of birth and death and of other minds and in our self-consciousness. Ultimately, such tensions are reducible to the paradox of being a person. The person is the concrete manifestation of a philosophical point of view, and whatever contradiction is inherent in the point of view is inherent in the person as well. Also, the absoluteness of the point of view is correlative to the unity of the person. By "absoluteness" here I mean the character of the point of view by virtue of which the person who holds it cannot imagine any alternative to it. This character is obviously connected with the fact that as fully actual the person cannot change. His full actuality consists in his maintenance of a point of view to which he sees no alternative. What we find most shocking when we greet a man whom we have not seen for some years is not that our friend has acquired gray hair or gained weight but that his point of view has changed. "He's not the same person at all!" we exclaim. What has happened strikes us as totally inexplicable. Indeed, it *is* a miracle when a person changes his mind with regard to fundamental philosophical issues. The change can have come about only because he was touched by some encounter or relationship that would not have touched another person at all.

I have said that the self arises only in a person both willing to admit that he has contradicted himself and committed to the standard of consistent discourse. This statement may seem to suggest that one can come to rest in a permanent contradiction permanently evoking the self. But no contradiction can be permanent; for it is part of the meaning of any contradiction that it is to be overcome. Whatever we are willing to settle for in perpetuity cannot be a contradiction—or else, in settling for it, we are in fact evading it. If a contradiction exists to be overcome, then we must take steps to overcome it. To illustrate such a movement, let me return to my example. The philosopher who holds that undetectable cases of color-blindness are possible has contradicted himself, as is revealed by the *argumentum ad hominem* addressed against him. Therefore there are no undetectable cases of color-blindness. But this view, too, is vulnerable to an *argumentum ad hominem*. If color-blindness is to be exhaustively defined by the public criteria in terms of which we can detect it, then neither color-blindness nor color-sensitivity has any subjective counterpart. Each is wholly a matter of a person's behavior, not of anything that might be said to be present to his mind or absent from it. But on the same principle, the meaning of any term referring to a mental state must be exhausted by publicly observable behavior. Hence if the philosopher says that he believes that there are no undetectable cases of color-blindness, he is only reporting his own behavior. However, while a belief can be true or false, behavior cannot. Yet surely he supposes his belief to be true. (Lovejoy called this contradiction "The Paradox of the Thinking Behaviorist."[13])

13. "The Paradox of the Thinking Behaviorist," *Philosophical Review*, Vol. 31, 1922, pp. 135–47.

The possibility of making a philosophical claim evaporates in the panobjectivism implicit in the verificationist's view, just as it does in the pansubjectivism implicit in the view of his rival that undetectable cases of color-blindness are possible.

So far we have not taken any forward step of the kind that I said is necessary to overcome the contradiction. There is no one uniquely required step. But a step that would be possible at this point is to declare that the objectivity and subjectivity of color-blindness are conditions for each other. Unless color-blindness had a public meaning, it might be contended, it could not have a private meaning. Nothing can be undetectable unless we know what that thing is of which it is the criterion.

We have arrived at a dialectical view of color-blindness. As a philosophical view, it is certain to have its own defects. But these are not the defects of either of the views from which it has emerged. They represent novelty. Progress has been made. Although we face a new contradiction, it is one that results from the overcoming of an old one.

I conclude this book by outlining a second example of philosophical conflict that gives rise to the self. This example is quite different from the one with which I have been occupied thus far. The difference between the examples may help to suggest the ubiquity of the phenomenon. The second example, furthermore, helps to elucidate the motto I have used for the book as a whole.

The example is Hegel's conception of an "unhappy consciousness." In the *Phenomenology of Spirit* Hegel shows how this consciousness arises. We need not trace out all of its antedecents for it can be sufficiently explained in terms of its emergence from Hegel's version of Skepticism. Skepticism, as presented at this stage of the Phenomenology, is a radical rejection of every metaphysical distinction, such as the distinction, for example, between form and content, between the teleological and the mechanical, between knowledge and opinion, or between primary and secondary qualities. "Such a distinction," says Hegel, "has nothing permanent in it, and *must* disappear before thinking, because the distinct is precisely what is not in itself but has its essentiality in another."[14] What Hegel has in mind is that any distinction presupposes a criterion in terms of which it can be carried out. But the criterion

14. In the passages that follow, I have made my own translations from *Phänomenologie des Geistes*, B IV B.

falls outside the distinction—it cannot be established by that very distinction of which it is the criterion. Thus if we claim that there is an ultimate distinction between form and content, we must back that claim up by stating *how* form and content are to be distinguished—by naming the criterion of the distinction. Perhaps we shall say "The form of anything is the way in which it functions in the system in which it occurs; while its content is any property of a thing that is irrelevant to the way in which it functions." Or we might say "The form of anything is the way in which we know it. Its content is anything about it that is irrelevant to our knowledge of it." In either case, we are making explicit a criterion of form presupposed by the distinction between form and content. If we could not make any such criterion explicit, we would have no right to make the distinction; and naturally the criterion must lie outside the distinction; for if we were to attempt to formulate the criterion in terms of the distinction itself—for example by defining form as function and then attempting to formulate function as the way in which a thing exhibits its form—we would be involved in a vicious circle. Thus "the distinct is precisely what is not in itself but has its essentiality in another." In other words, every distinction is arbitrary.

Hegel now shows that there is a contradiction in this skeptical denial of the ultimacy of each and every distinction. For on the one hand, as we continue to exhibit the arbitrariness of one distinction after another we cannot avoid the awareness that it is we who have made the distinctions in the first place. Thus our activity in making them is completely random and irresponsible; we set up and knock down distinctions as a child arbitrarily sets up and knocks down towers of blocks.

On the other hand, "Just as consciousness evaluates itself in this way as an individual, accidental, and . . . lost self-consciousness, it makes itself on the contrary once again a universal self-identity: for it is the negativity . . . of every distinction." In other words, our very repudiation of our own work as arbitrary presupposes a nonarbitrary basis of judgment. Yet this newly acquired confidence is short-lived. For what could such a nonarbitrary basis of judgment be? If every distinction is arbitrary, then the distinction between a nonarbitrary basis of judgment and an arbitrary one is itself arbitrary. Hence "From this self-identity, . . . [consciousness] again collapses into contingency and disorder."

The vacillation between our view of ourselves as authors of an altogether arbitrary piece of work and our view of ourselves as sound judges of our own deficiencies can be represented more schematically as follows. Suppose I doubt a metaphysical position. Then the doubt itself presupposes a metaphysical position. But that position is altogether arbitrary. Yet the judgment that it is arbitrary presupposes some independent basis of judgment. But that basis is altogether arbitrary. Yet the judgment that . . .

Hence the vacillation can never come to rest. We may picture Hegel's skeptic as a man who is continually changing his mind about his own status. At one moment he is on top of the world, for he sees himself as the judge of all distinctions. At the next moment he is on the abyss of despair, because he sees that his own judgment must be arbitrary. At a third moment he has climbed out this abyss.

We do no injustice to the vacillation of a skeptic if we think of his utterances as constituting a dialogue between two persons. We can picture the dialogue as "a quarrel between stubborn youths of whom one says A when the other says B, and B when the other says A, and each of whom, by contradicting himself, achieves the satisfaction of remaining in contradiction with the other." The fact that the vacillation can be represented as a dialogue shows that the skeptic is not being altogether honest with himself. His skepticism "keeps the poles of [its] contradiction apart from one another." It does this by representing these poles as successive in time—as serially ordered ups and downs. But the truth of the matter is that the poles exist simultaneously in one and the same act of consciousness. For it is not one man who judges and another who declares the judgment of his partner to be arbitrary; it is in fact one man who does both. Hence the contradiction cannot be averted by spreading it out in time. It exists all at once. And its existence is painful. The consciousness that is aware of harboring it is an "Unhappy Consciousness." What Hegel calls an "Unhappy Conscious" I would call a self.

The skeptic can accept the view that all judgments are arbitrary without supposing that it is his self which has accepted this view; he can later accept the view that at least one judgment is not arbitrary without supposing that it is his self which has accepted this view. In neither case is there anything in his experience capable of evoking or revealing a self; if the skeptic says simply "I accept this view," all is in order just as it stands. The experience of accepting either view is transparent; it raises no questions that need to be answered in terms of a self.

The transparency of the skeptic's experience is the result of a dissimulation and an evasion of responsibility. For *in fact* it is from a single point of view that the skeptic has accepted both "all judgments are arbitrary" and "at least one judgment is not arbitrary." If he can somehow be brought to see this, the situation will radically change. All is no longer in order just as it stands. A contradiction has appeared, and must be accounted for. One way of accounting for a contradiction is to make a distinction that will dissolve it. But it is obvious that any such distinction would simply be a return to skepticism. To say that while from one point of view all judgments are arbitrary, from another at least one judgment is not arbitrary, is to engage in exactly the same dissimulation that resulted in a temporal spread. The account of the contradiction must be more fundamental than this. It must not deny the status of the contradiction as a contradiction. It is this more fundamental account of the contradiction that evokes the self. The self is evoked as the locus of the contradiction. To put the matter in another way: the presence of the contradiction is felt as a burden, and the self emerges to take up this burden—or perhaps it is more accurate to say that the self *is* the taking up of the burden. There is no similar burden in the acceptance of any noncontradictory position.

When a contradiction occurs, the self can emerge to accept responsibility for it. Yet in the absence of the self there could be no contradiction—there could be no more than a skeptical alternation of poles. The self is the consciousness, unified for the first time, in which the contradiction appears. Thus the relation between self and contradiction is reciprocal. Contradiction, which calls the self into existence, presupposes that the self has already juxtaposed the contradictory poles.

INDEX